WHAT WE DO NOW

WHAT WE DO NOW

EDITED BY
LEOPOLD FROEHLICH

MELVILLE HOUSE
BROOKLYN • LONDON

What We Do Now : Standing Up for Democracy in America
First published in 2026 by Melville House

Edited by Leopold Froehlich

First Melville House Printing: August 2025
Distributed by Penguin Random House LLC, 1745
Broadway, New York, NY 10019 USA.
www.penguinrandomhouse.com

Melville House Publishing
46 John Street
Brooklyn, NY 11201
and
Melville House UK
Suite 2000
16/18 Woodford Road
London E7 0HA

mhpbooks.com
@melvillehouse

ISBN: 978-1-68589-271-5
ISBN: 978-1-68589-272-2 (eBook)

Library of Congress Control Number: 2026939626

Designed by Beste M. Doğan

Printed in the United States of America
10 9 8 7 6 5 4 3 2 1

A catalog record for this book is available from the Library of Congress

INTRODUCTION

LEOPOLD FROEHLICH

ONCE AGAIN, THE NOBLE AMERICAN SYSTEM has failed. Institutions didn't protect us from tyranny and our heroes were ineffective. The sacred Constitution didn't magically intervene, and our better natures did not prevail. The guardrails that we were told would confine lawlessness were broken-down; we were assured that norms would save us, that basic human decencies would overrule brigandry.

Instead, we have virtual lawlessness, a poke in the eye, grift, corruption, stupidity, emolument, someone shot in broad daylight on Fifth Avenue while the triumphant shooter strolls away, waving and grinning. It would be farcical if so many hadn't suffered.

We've seen much hatred and violence since the start of 2025. "There is a lot of sadism and malice in all of us," the philosopher Richard Rorty noted, "waiting to be released when the social bond is loosened." Rorty defined sadism as "the use of persons weaker than ourselves as outlets for our resentments and frustrations, and especially for the infliction of pain."

Concern for a looming climate crisis has fallen into disfavor. Laws no longer matter, except in rare street-level incidents. The Fourth Estate has been muzzled. Righteous indignation at the ravages of technology and inhuman systems is no longer deemed worthy of public attention. Madness and idiocy and ugliness have brought us to the (constant) brink of extinction, and reward us with the appalling cage-fighting spectacle of bread and circus that is our government.

How are we to respond to what Gerald Ford, in quainter times, referred to as "our long national nightmare"? We need solidarity, most of all. We must respect our communities and stand together. And we need solutions, reparations. So, what is to be done?

This book contains eighteen essays, from abstract to praxis. They offer the reader both practical advice and theoretical structure. From Bernie Sanders's call for a nationwide grassroots movement to Sarah Jaffe's essay on the appropriate nature of grieving, *What We Do Now* provides hope, if not solace. We can take back our country.

We have not yet begun to fight. In the words of Tom Paine: "Let it be told to the future world, that in the depth of winter, when nothing but hope and virtue could survive, that the city and the country, alarmed at one common danger, came forth to meet and to repulse it."

This is our country. Let our voices be heard. Let's go to the streets and stand up.

WHAT WE DO NOW

REVERSE AMERICA'S DECLINE

IT IS NOT GOOD ENOUGH JUST TO CRITICIZE TRUMP

BERNIE SANDERS

AT THIS DIFFICULT MOMENT IN AMERICAN history, it's imperative that we have the courage to be honest with ourselves.

The United States, once the envy of the world, is now a nation in profound decline. For the sake of our children and future generations, we must reverse that decline and change, in very fundamental ways, the direction of our country.

Not so long ago, the US was admired for its democracy, constitution, rule of law, strong middle class and an American dream which promised that our kids and grandchildren would have a better life than their parents.

Tragically, that is no longer the case.

We used to have the strongest and most vibrant middle class on Earth. Not any more. Today 60% of our people are living paycheck to paycheck and we have more income and wealth inequality than any other major country. Despite huge advances in technology and worker productivity, real weekly wages for the average American worker are lower today than they were 53 years ago.

We used to be the best-educated country on Earth, with an excellent public school system and the highest percentage of young people graduating from college than any other country. Not any more. Today, the US ranks well behind its peers in overall educational attainment, our childcare system is broken and millions of our young people are unable to afford a college education.

We used to have the best healthcare system in the world. Not any more. Despite spending far more per capita on healthcare than any other nation, 85 million Americans are uninsured or underinsured, our life expectancy is lower than most wealthy nations and we have a massive shortage in doctors, nurses, dentists, mental health counselors and other healthcare professionals.

We used to be a country with decent, affordable housing. Not any more. Since the pandemic, the median home price has risen by 55% to more than $410,000. Today, more than 20 million households are spending more than half of their limited incomes on housing and nearly 800,000 people are homeless. Today, young couples are buying their first home, on average, 10 years later in life than their parents.

We used to have a reasonably nutritious food system. Not any more. Today, as a result of corporate agriculture and the greed of the food and beverage industry, many of our kids are addicted to ultra-processed foods and we have the highest rate of obesity and diabetes of any major country on Earth.

We used to have the most advanced transportation system in the world. Not any more. Our public transportation and rail systems lag far behind most other developed countries and millions of people spend hours a day in traffic jams.

But the decline we are seeing in our country is not just in economics. Our political system is corrupt, dominated by an extremely greedy billionaire class that is able to buy and sell politicians.

Even more troubling, our country is rapidly descending into authoritarianism under an unstable, narcissistic leader who wants more and more power for himself.

Donald Trump is usurping the powers of Congress, attacking the courts, intimidating the media, threatening universities, and prosecuting and arresting his political opponents.

We are living through one of the most difficult moments in the history of our country And then, on top of all that, there is Trump's domestic army, ICE, an agency which, every day, is acting in outrageous and unconstitutional ways.

ICE is occupying and terrorizing communities, kicking down doors without due process, sending five-year-old children to detention centers, illegally deporting people and shooting down American citizens in cold blood.

Further, Trump's authoritarianism extends far beyond our own borders.

Today, we have a president who feels far more comfortable with the dictatorships of Saudi Arabia, Qatar and the UAE than with the democratic nations in Europe, a president who, along with Elon Musk and others, is supporting rightwing extremist parties throughout the world.

We have a president who has given unconditional support to the Israeli prime minister, Benjamin Netanyahu, a war criminal who is under indictment by the international criminal court for his genocidal policies.

We have a president who violates international law with impunity by illegally attacking Venezuela, absurdly suggesting that Canada become our 51st state and, insanely, threatening to seize Greenland from Denmark.

So where do we go from here? How do we reverse America's decline? How do we create an economy that works for working people and not just billionaires, a vibrant democracy and a foreign policy based on international law?

The answer is not complicated. We do it by building a national grassroots movement that fights for the needs of the American working class. We do it by bringing people together – Black, white, Latino, Asian, gay and straight

– around an agenda that takes on the greed of the oligarchs and is based on the foundation of economic, social, racial and environmental justice.

Is this an impossible dream? Can it be done? You bet it can.

Zohran Mamdani's successful grassroots campaign in New York City has given us the roadmap.

Starting at just 1% in the polls, Mamdani had the guts to take on the Democratic establishment, the Republican establishment and the oligarchs. And he won by organizing a grassroots campaign of more than 90,000 volunteers knocking on doors behind a strong progressive agenda.

Yes. What Mamdani accomplished in New York City can and should be replicated in all 50 states.

The lesson of Mamdani's campaign is clear: it is not good enough just to be critical of Trump and his destructive policies. We must bring forth a positive vision that will improve the lives of ordinary Americans.

Here are just a few of the issues that must be addressed:

We must create a vibrant democracy by ending Citizens United and preventing billionaires from buying elections.

Whether the Democratic establishment likes it or not,

we must guarantee healthcare as a human right through Medicare for All.

We must build millions of affordable homes and apartments and give our younger generation the opportunity to own a home of their own.

We must make public colleges, universities, trade schools and medical schools tuition-free and have the best childcare and public school system in the entire world.

We must expand social security and bring back traditional pension plans so that every senior in this country can retire with dignity.

We must raise the minimum wage to a living wage and guarantee every worker the right to join a union.

We must demand that the wealthiest people and most profitable corporations in America pay their fair share in taxes.

We are living through one of the most difficult moments in the history of our country. But the truth is that, throughout our nation's history, we have faced great challenges before. From the Revolutionary War to the abomination of slavery, from the Great Depression to the Second World War, and from the century-long struggle for civil rights to the struggles for women's rights, workers' rights and LGBTQ+ rights, the people of our nation fought for justice – and prevailed. And we can do it again.

In times of great crisis, the American people came together and chose democracy over authoritarianism, justice over greed, solidarity over division. They understood in the past – and we understand today – that when we stand together, no matter how much money and power the oligarchs have, there is nothing that we cannot accomplish.

That is how we reverse America's decline, renew our democracy, and build a future worthy of our children and generations yet to come.

CONTINUE TO RESIST

REMEMBER WE HAVE THE POWER TO MAKE OUR FUTURE

REBECCA SOLNIT

WHEN WE TALK ABOUT OPPOSITION IN POL-itics, sometimes it's just a policy disagreement—but in the current political crisis in the US, the opposition has become the opposite of the Trump administration in meaningful ways. It had to because this is not only a policy conflict.

Between the administration and the opposition are actual opposites of principle: among those committed to inclusion and those to exclusion; truth and lies; kindness and cruelty; the protection and destruction of systems that in turn protect the climate or public health.

It seems possible that what will ultimately emerge is a clarified sense of principles and a deeper commitment to them (which is why part of the conflict is over American history itself).

On one hand, there are the heads of the federal government and their spokespeople, whose lies are part of their disdain for the electorate and the rule of law. Those lies also get served up as the justification for their cruelty—the cruelty directed toward federal workers, immigrants, children in this country in need of food and healthcare, including vaccines, and the millions of people currently starving or devastated by preventable disease around the world since Elon Musk's "department of government efficiency" gang destroyed USAID.

Politicians' lies were once decried and punished when detected, in a process that often led to contriteness and apologies from the liar. Even the act of lying was a furtive one when people feared detection and its consequences. Now lies are the backbone of the Trump administration's utterances—from likely lying about the inhabitants of the small boats they are blowing up in the Caribbean, to lying about vaccines, the economy, climate, polls, laws, history, race, immigration and pretty much everything else.

White House press secretary Karoline Leavitt specializes in grotesque falsehoods in praise of Donald Trump's health, intelligence, success, and popularity. Robert F. Kennedy Jr., the health and human services secretary, peddles lies about health and healthcare and the science behind them. Vice President JD Vance has likewise lied about a broad range of subjects, but his venom has been particularly directed at immigrants, who he falsely accuses of dire economic impacts and outlandish crimes. White House adviser Stephen Miller has told the same lies with even more venom. But Trump is first and last the liar-in-chief.

It's clear that many on the far right are now part of a subculture that celebrates and revels in cruelty and viciousness and doesn't mind dishonesty. Trump officials sometimes seem baffled by the response from the rest of us who aren't part of it, but apparently they don't think we matter. We're not their target audience, and this indifference to the opinion and values of the majority is itself a testament to their commitment to minority rule. It's our job as the opposition to matter. And we have.

The immigrant-rights opposition is motivated by solidarity with those under attack, underwritten by compassion. From Los Angeles to Chicago to Charlotte, North Carolina, people have risked their own physical and legal safety to stand with those under attack by Immigration and Customs Enforcement (ICE), and organized, trained and otherwise done the work to protect their neighbors. It has had a major impact on the ability of ICE to persecute immigrants and the Brown and Black people whose immigration status doesn't seem to matter to these goon squads—sometimes as specific as preventing a person from being hauled away, sometimes as broad as the unprecedented protests this year.

For example, the *Chicago Tribune* reports that on October 25, "agents deployed even more tear gas, this time right before a children's Halloween parade in Irving Park, where a resident raced out of his house, still in his Chicago Blackhawks pajamas, to confront feds who'd tackled a man in his front yard."

Others, as lawyers, judges, protesters, journalists, scientists and educators, have defended truth, facts, science and law to protect human beings and the social and natural systems we depend on. They have stood up for the authority of truth that authoritarians seek to squelch or corrupt. The withholding and corrupting of information by the administration is corrosive to democracy, and it comes from a kind of elitism that regards the rest of us as not deserving the truth—and maybe suckers who will buy the lies (which plenty on the right actually are, and most of the rest of us aren't).

Facts, truth, science, history are themselves democratic. The causes of the civil war, Covid-19 and the climate crisis are the same whether you're a billionaire or a busker, and money can't buy you out of that—though it can buy you a social media platform or a network news corporation to corrupt.

The opposition has been marked most of all by solidarity (which is by definition alliance and commitment to those who are not the same as you), an embrace of difference. I do not believe there has been anything like this level of solidarity with immigrants and refugees before, from the crowds showing up in the streets to the US senator who flew to El Salvador to try to rescue the kidnapped and persecuted Kilmar Ábrego García. I hope that it gives rise to a shift in the Democratic party's discourse about immigrants and refugees, from a watered-down acceptance of their characterization as a burden and a problem, to recognition of their irreplaceable contributions to this country, economically and otherwise.

The attempts to secure truth and maybe justice for Jeffrey Epstein's victims has also been driven by solidarity with the victims and a sense of principle that the Trump administration and Trump himself don't share. Their victimization was the result of the radical inequality between poor girls and young women and wealthy men, so one of the underlying questions is about equality, about whether we will have a nation in which everyone's rights matter, in which everyone deserves protection by the law.

It has been remarkable how this scandal that refuses to die down was what caused widespread Republican defection, when members of the House and Senate voted so broadly to release the files and some Republicans spoke openly against Trump himself. Polls show Trump's own popularity and that of his handling of the economy and immigration has declined radically over the course of the year.

It was not clear when 2025 began what kind of opposition to the Trump administration there would be and how effective it would be. Many at the beginning of the year feared a powerful administration whose destruction went unchallenged, but it has been challenged and it has stumbled, faltered and backed down in many situations.

The administration now seems to be getting more extreme and reckless as it grows more desperate, chaotic and unpopular. We entered 2026 with radical uncertainty about the fate of this country—but also with the clarity that people have the power to determine what it will be, if they continue to show up and stand on principle.

ACT NOW

ONE YEAR OF TRUMP: THE TIME TO ACT IS NOW, WHILE WE STILL CAN

M. GESSEN

A YEAR INTO DONALD TRUMP'S SECOND term, friends who live outside the United States continue to express shock at the news that comes from this country, often mixed with concern for my safety. I shrug. Even those of us in the United States who oppose this administration's actions have a way of normalizing them. On Tuesday, I saw a news release in my inbox: A new filing in the legal case against the construction of the giant immigrant detention facility in Florida. I—like many other Americans, it seems—had almost forgotten about Alligator Alcatraz.

In Europe, attention has been unwavering. Journalists are writing articles and making documentaries about America building a concentration camp. On these shores, we have simply become a country that builds concentration camps. It's only one of the changes we have absorbed in the last year.

We have become a country where people are disappeared by a paramilitary force that hunts them down in their apartments, on city streets and country roads, and even in the courts. Less than a year ago, videos of ICE arrests would go viral and social media posts about ICE sightings would send chills down our spines. Now even the most high-profile detentions have faded from view: Who has been released? Who has been deported? Who is still missing?

Who can keep track?

We have become a country where a person can be summarily executed in public for protesting that paramilitary force. After an ICE agent killed Renee Good by shooting her three times at point-blank range in Minneapolis on Jan. 7, President Trump, Vice President JD Vance and other federal officials said the shooting was justified as an act of self-defense (the video shows otherwise) and pointed to Good's ostensible affiliation with left-wing groups—apparently affirming that protest is now punishable by death in America.

We have become a country whose federal government deploys military and paramilitary forces in the streets of its major cities, terrorizing the residents in the guise of protecting them. A foreign observer taking stock of the United States could describe us as a nation on the brink of civil war. But we can barely keep current the list of cities where troops have been or still are in the streets: Washington, D.C.; Los Angeles; Chicago; Portland, Ore.; Memphis; New Orleans. The number of armed federal agents deployed to Minneapolis may now be five times the size of the city's police force.

We have become a country whose government is attacking its universities, defunding research, reversing scientific advances, assaulting museums and hollowing out cultural institutions. Few of these attacks—carried out in broad daylight, announced in executive orders, extolled in speeches and put on display in giant metal letters—meet meaningful resistance. We are making ourselves stupider.

We have become a country that demonstratively tramples on international laws. Our military bombs a different nation every few weeks, commits murder on the high seas and removes foreign political leaders by force. Our government threatens the world, including our allies, with its imperial ambitions.

We are a country ruled by a megalomaniac whose views are openly hateful and proudly ignorant, whose avarice knows no bounds and whose claim to power is absolute. Foreign leaders try to appease him with flattery and curry his favor with gifts. It rarely works to temper his appetite or even catch his attention, but it's seemingly all they can do.

To be sure, some elements of our current condition predate Trump. This country has long maintained the world's largest carceral system, and one of the least humane in the Western world; it formed the foundation for the concentration camps. Police executions of Black people have long been a pattern. The origins of ICE and its parent agency, the Department of Homeland Security, conceived as a secret police force, go back to 9/11. The culture wars date to at least the 1980s. And disregarding international law, playing the world's heavily armed policeman, has been a longstanding bipartisan tradition — as have increasingly hostile, restrictive immigration policies. The presidency itself has been growing less transparent and more powerful for at least a couple of decades.

I am not arguing that what we have become this year is just more of the same. Few people would make this argument anymore. But the truth is, even though we are taught to think of history as a series of definitive turning points with specific dates — wars, revolutions, assassinations, declarations of independence and decrees announcing martial law — no transformation is instant or total. This Trump administration has moved at breakneck speed. And still, it hasn't broken everything yet.

We are still a country with a robust civil society. The lawyers have fought the administration in court. The people have rallied against Trump's usurpation of power and have organized to protect their neighbors from ICE. But Trump's attacks on universities, his assault on the judiciary, and his threats against nonprofits and philanthropies have already altered the way civil society functions. The universities and the foundations aren't what they were a year ago, and neither is the judiciary, where so much civil-society work is concentrated. And the execution of Renee Good has surely affected every potential protester's mental calculus.

We still have independent media. But taking stock of how much the media landscape has changed is sobering. Even before the 2024 election, the owners of the *Washington Post* and the *Los Angeles Times* curtailed the independence of their editorial pages. Soon after the election, ABC News and then the parent company of CBS News paid millions of dollars to settle what certainly appeared to be frivolous lawsuits filed by Trump. (He has filed several more, including one against the *New York Times*, and another against 20 individual members of the Pulitzer Prize Board, which includes *Times* journalists.) Now, under new ownership, CBS is rapidly transforming itself into a Trump-friendly network.

Autocrats destroy the free press in at least two ways: by cracking down, as Trump has done through lawsuits and regulatory pressure, and by reapportioning access to information. In October, the Trump administration effectively kicked legacy media outlets out of the Pentagon, replacing them with loyal journalists and influencers. The media, like civil society, is much diminished compared with what it was a year ago.

We still have elections. But how free and fair will the 2026 elections be? Trump doesn't just carry a grudge against the election authorities of many states; he made that grudge a centerpiece of his 2024 campaign. Since he returned to office, his administration has taken a series of executive actions and filed a series of lawsuits aimed at restricting access to the polls, purging voter rolls, limiting the independence of local election authorities, and generally laying the groundwork for the systematic intimidation of both voters and election officials. States have joined this effort. Florida is cracking down on voter registration drives. Ohio and other states have introduced restrictive voter ID laws. Georgia has limited poll hours and banned providing food or water to people standing in line to vote. Texas has gerrymandered a map that threatens to disenfranchise Black and Latino voters and may wipe five

Democratic congressional seats out of existence, and the Supreme Court has allowed this controversial new map to be used in the 2026 midterms. Add to this Trump's threat to deploy the military to deal with the "enemy from within" during the elections on the one hand and his promise to send Americans what amounts to a bribe—$2,000 checks "toward the end of the year" — and you have the prospect of elections that are far less free and a lot less fair than the last ones.

As for the next presidential election, Trump has made his intentions clear: He is not planning to leave his throne. He may look for a pretext to cancel the vote. (When President Volodymyr Zelensky told him that Ukraine can't have an election during the war, Trump visibly lit up: "So you mean if we happen to be in a war with somebody, no more elections? Oh, that's good.") He may find a way to invalidate the vote after the election — he has been laying the groundwork for such a move since his first term. Even if he doesn't, it is foolish to think that this iteration of our national nightmare will end in three years.

One term for regimes that maintain the trappings of democracy, such as legislatures, courts and elections, but use them primarily as decoration is "electoral authoritarianism." This is what we are becoming.

It matters what we call things—what we call ourselves. It matters for wonky reasons like reading the polls: Public opinion functions differently in democratic and nondemocratic societies. But it matters more for how we think about the future. We can't count on change being brought about by elections when we can't count on elections. We can't count on the freedoms and resources we enjoy today to still be available to us tomorrow.

Ask any people who have lived in a country that became an autocracy, and they will tell you some version of a story about walls closing in on them, about space getting smaller and smaller. The space they are talking about is freedom. In Russia, mass protest used to be possible. (The first time people got prison terms for peaceful protest, in 2012, I wrote a whole book about it.) Then mass protest became impossible and the only option was what we called the one-person picket: a person standing alone with a sign. Then people started getting arrested for standing alone with a blank piece of paper, then for "liking" something on social media. Russian journalists used to know that they could write freely as long as they stuck to culture and avoided politics; now a person can get arrested for performing a tune by a banned songwriter.

Of course, the United States is not Russia—or Hungary or Venezuela or Israel or any of the many other democracies that have turned or are turning themselves into autocracies. But now is the time to focus on the similarities and try to learn from the ways other countries have cracked down on protest, eviscerated their electoral systems, limited their media freedom and built concentration camps. The only way to keep the space from imploding is to fill it, to prop up the walls: to claim all the room there still is for speaking, writing, publishing, protesting, voting. It's what the people of Minnesota appear to be doing, and it's something each of us needs to do—right now, while we still can.

FIGHT BACK

FROM MINNEAPOLIS TO "BREAD AND ROSES," WORKERS HAVE ALWAYS FOUGHT BACK

KIM KELLY

ON JANUARY 23, 2026, THE PEOPLE OF Minneapolis zipped up their coats, pulled on their snow boots, and took to the streets. Tens of thousands of Minnesotans answered the call of "no work, no school, no shopping" and joined in a statewide day of protest. Their loudest demand was simple: for the 3,000 Immigration and Customs Enforcement (ICE) agents currently occupying the North Star State to get the hell out.

Some referred to the action as an "economic blackout," the "Day of Truth & Freedom," while others took inspiration from the city's own vibrant labor history and dubbed it a general strike. No matter how you slice it, everyday operations in the Twin Cities screeched to a halt that day. Hundreds of businesses and cultural institutions closed, workers walked off the job, students walked out of school; praying clergy and faith leaders blocked the road to the Minneapolis–St. Paul airport, and the Minnesota AFL-CIO, the state's federation of more than 1,000 affiliated local unions, encouraged its members to join the afternoon march.

Organizers also called for Jonathan Ross, the ICE agent who fatally shot 37-year-old mother of three Renee Nicole Good, to be held accountable; an end to federal funding increases for ICE; and for Minnesota corporations to cease cooperating with the agency. "After weeks of living under the heavy weight of this racist campaign of terror by ICE agents . . . today we are going to show our power," Kieran Knutson, president of the Communications Workers of America Local 7250 in Minneapolis, told *Democracy Now!*

Earlier this month, the Trump administration sent thousands of ICE agents to the Minneapolis-St. Paul area to launch a large-scale immigration raid on the local Somali community. Since then, the agency's poorly trained, heavily armed officers have wreaked havoc in the area, tear-gassing and assaulting residents, including US citizens; detaining small children; harassing elders; and brutally killing two people—Good, and 37-year-old ICU nurse Alex Pretti.

In 2020, police officer Derek Chauvin murdered Minneapolis resident George Floyd in broad daylight, sparking a protest movement that swept through the entire country. Minneapolis hasn't forgotten what they learned about organizing and rebellion during that fiery summer, and as ICE began disappearing their friends and neighbors, that muscle memory kicked in. Citywide mutual aid networks, ICE watch groups, food distribution, and deep community care have defined the locals' response to ICE's occupation, even as the agents themselves have relied on violence and aggression to try to stamp out resistance. When January 23 came, the temperatures dropped well below zero but the streets filled with thousands upon thousands of people, armed with only their signs, their families, and their hand warmers.

I was over a thousand miles away that day, and could only follow the action via social media and texts from friends. As workers in Minneapolis put down their tools and hit the streets, I was walking around frigid Lawrence, MA, with a group of labor organizers from around the country, taking in the history of a much older work stoppage: the 1912 Bread and Roses Strike. That was another cold, wintry, citywide labor action led by immigrant workers and their allies, inspired by a fight for dignity and justice, sustained by mutual aid, and marred by police violence.

The early 1900s were a period of intense xenophobia and anti-immigrant sentiment, and factory bosses took advantage of the widespread discrimination to pay their predominantly foreign-born workforces next to nothing. In the thunderous textile mills of Lawrence, thousands of mostly young women and children labored under dirty, humid conditions to churn out endless yards of cotton and woolen cloth; accidents were common, and tuberculosis and pneumonia were a constant threat.

"Thirty-six of every 100 of all men and women who

work in the mills die before or by the time they are 25 years of age," Dr. Elizabeth Shapleigh, a Lawrence physician, wrote in a 1912 study. Girls as young as 14 worked up to 56 hours per week, while making pennies on the dollar; adult workers with families to support struggled to feed their children on their tiny wages. When mill owners cut workers' hours from 56 to 54 hours per week, they also cut those two hours' worth of pay—32 cents a week, the price of several loaves of bread—from their paychecks. For workers who were bringing home less than $9 per six-day week, that lost bread was the last straw.

On January 11, 1912, Polish women weavers at the Everett Mill walked off the job in protest. Word of the action quickly spread, and within a week they'd been joined by 25,000 others. Lawrence was an incredibly diverse city with a large immigrant population that hailed from 51 different countries, and the strike saw Italian, Lithuanian, Polish, Irish, Russian, French, Portuguese, Armenian, Syrian, Lebanese, and Palestinian workers all join together for the cause.

As the strike went on, organizers from the worker-led Industrial Workers of the World (IWW) union and the

Italian Socialist Federation helped the strikers form committees, raise money, and rally public support as the strike stretched into its second month. Meanwhile, local women joined the picket lines and fought cops, as well as running strike kitchens. They needed all the help they could get: City officials had responded to the strike by calling in the local militia and using police to harass and intimidate workers on the picket lines.

When strikers fought back, they were beaten or jailed; when organizers arranged to send strikers' children out of the city to stay with pro-union families, cops attacked their train, dragging women and children off the platform and causing one woman to miscarry. Public sympathy soon swung in the workers' direction, and Camella Teoli, a 14-year-old mill girl who had been scalped when her long hair got swept up in a textile machine, was invited to testify at a Congressional hearing in March 1912. By the end of the month, American Woolen Company and the other struck mills had caved. The workers won a 15 percent wage increase, double pay for overtime, and a pledge not to retaliate against workers who'd taken part in the strike. Fearful of being hit by work stoppages of their own, mill owners across New England also adopted many of the strikers' demands.

The tactics used by young immigrant women to take on Lawrence's textile barons are still in use today worldwide. They held multilingual meetings to ensure every worker felt heard and represented, and translated their publications into 25 languages. They cooked and fed one another, organizing soup kitchens and putting produce donations from local farmers to good use. They defended one another in the face of state violence and police brutality, and above all else, they refused to allow themselves to be divided.

"All the nations of the world are represented in this fight of the workers for more bread," the strikers stated in a public proclamation that was translated into multiple languages and shared. "The flaxen-haired son of the North marches side by side with his dark-haired brother of the South. They have toiled together in the factory for one boss. And now they have joined together in a great cause, and they have cast aside all racial and religious prejudice for the common good, determined to win a victory over the greed of the corrupt, unfeeling mill owners, who have ruled these people so long with the whip of hunger and the lash of the unemployed."

In short, they won because of solidarity—which is also exactly how the people of Minnesota built the durable and inspiring resistance network we all saw on January 23. Where strikers once relied on word of mouth, alarm bells, and mass meetings, today's rebels have now added Signal chats, whistles, and affinity groups to their organizing toolbox. Times and conditions may change, but the struggle between labor and capital continues.

"The crimes of the police during this trouble are almost beyond human imagination," the textile workers wrote all those years ago. "They have clubbed the strikers at every opportunity. They have dragged little children from their mothers' arms and with their clubs they have struck women who are in a state of pregnancy. They have placed people under arrest for no reason whatsoever." Does that sound familiar? These early 20th-century mill girls may as well have been describing ICE. Lawrence remains a city of immigrants, where more than 80 percent of the population is Latino. Decades of migration from Puerto Rico and the Dominican Republic have revitalized the old textile town, where mills have since been turned into condos. ICE has recently stepped up its raids there, leading to an uptick in arrests and detentions that has set the entire city on edge.

I was sad not to be able to stand with protesters in Minnesota that day, but spending time in Lawrence was a much-needed reminder that there have always been workers who fought back. They refused to swallow bigoted propaganda and abandon one another in times of crisis, stood up for the most vulnerable, and stared down danger when it came for them, because the alternative—giving up—was unimaginable. My little field trip ended in a parking lot somewhere in Boston, where hundreds of people—union members, immigrant-justice organizers, socialists, grandmas, and anyone else you can think of—rallied in 19-degree weather to show their solidarity with the people of Minneapolis and against ICE's vicious assault on our communities. It was beautiful, and it felt like yet another step toward the better future we all deserve.

We still have plenty to learn from those who came before us, including the workers, organizers, strikers, and everyday people who found the courage to stand up against injustice and refuse to accept the unacceptable.

Already, student unions in Minneapolis are calling for another mass work stoppage on January 30. As the workers of Lawrence said when they proudly walked out into the freezing January morning in 1912, "Great is the provocation, greater must be the answer of the workers to the employing class... On to the general strike of all workers, of all professions, of women, men, and children. Tie up everything. On to action!"

DEFEND DIVERSITY

THEY'RE NOT JUST COMING FOR DEI. THEY'RE COMING FOR DEMOCRACY

STACEY ABRAMS

THE TRUMP ADMINISTRATION HAS EXpanded its attacks on America's most vulnerable communities. From the horrific Republican tax and budget bill that plunges the working classes into debt and supercharges masked deportations, to the executive orders demonizing the homeless and prohibiting algorithmic justice in AI, Republicans have moved to eradicate their deepest fear: a multiracial, multiethnic democracy.

Republicans are implementing a blueprint to displace democracy with a government powered by Christian nationalism and techno-fascism. Conservative estimates count at least 10 million people having their healthcare ripped away. Immigrants are being stripped of due process, with a staggering $75 billion allocated to ICE over the next four years. While the unhoused and under-resourced are villainized, the richest will benefit from the largest generational wealth transfer in US history.

And it's not happening in isolation.

From the Supreme Court to state legislatures, cable news to college campuses, we're witnessing a coordinated campaign to undermine key pillars of American democracy. Its aim is clear: deny dignity, silence dissent, and dismantle progress—especially when it's led by women, people of color, immigrants, the disabled, LGBTQ+ communities, and the working poor.

Loaded terms like "waste, fraud, and abuse" are applied to disabled veterans navigating a broken system, but *not* to billionaires siphoning our data to feed AI. Politicians and pundits rail about tightened budgets, misplaced priorities, or "local control." But look closely—their favored policies claim neutrality but shift the burden to the most vulnerable.

The instinct is to see these as separate, concurrent attacks. Yet, modern history shows that when autocrats break democracy's back, they do it through complicity, civil service cuts, and unchecked expansions of power. And as democracy flails, the perpetrators must give the public a target for their despair.

The scapegoat of the moment is DEI.

Diversity, equity, and inclusion (DEI) initiatives have been attacked at lightning speed—from public universities to corporate boardrooms. Executive orders ban disability targets, states censor books on slavery and Native resistance, and candidates demonize transgender children in ads and speeches. What terrifies autocrats in formation is not the melange of community—it's the power we have when we build, fight, and rise together.

Destroying DEI has a clear motive: to stop Americans from seeking common cause. It's easier to target an acronym than admit our putative leaders don't believe Black and brown kids deserve to see themselves in the stories they learn. That slashing mental health support for

LGBTQ+ teens is more palatable than accepting their existence. That it's better to lose money than admit that diverse teams yield higher profits.

When we erase truth from classrooms, deny care, or strip legal identity, we don't just harm the intended targets. We hollow out democracy for us all.

Across the country, states are blocking knowledge, censoring history, and criminalizing honest teaching about race and gender. The mission of those who oppose DEI isn't safety—it's silence. Fallen democracies from Germany in the 1930s to Hungary today repeat the pattern: Autocracies must quash communities whose stories challenge the myth of a perfect past.

Healthcare has also become collateral damage in this assault. The Supreme Court's recent decision allowing hospitals to deny emergency abortion care—even when a pregnant woman's life is in danger—is a calculated blow to bodily autonomy. The same forces attacking DEI programs are stripping away reproductive rights, defunding community health clinics, and undermining the Affordable Care Act.

They frame this as fiscal responsibility or religious

liberty. It's a refusal to value lives outside a narrow definition of "deserving."

And then there's the unraveling of civil rights.

The court's rollback of voting rights, its embrace of "colorblind" legal reasoning, and its attacks on LGBTQ+ protections are not about fairness—they are about erasure. About removing the few tools we have left to level the playing field and pretending that history no longer shapes our present.

These decisions signal to millions of Americans: Your identity is negotiable, your rights conditional, your presence undesirable.

Meanwhile, Republicans are rapidly consolidating powers that will be hard to wrest back. Congressional calls for mass deportations and the sweeping criminalization of dissent are becoming features of America. These ideas may have seemed fringe once. Now they're at the heart of government policy.

Authoritarianism doesn't always look like a coup. It can arrive through a slower drip of cruel intentions dressed up as common sense. Not tanks in the streets (though we have seen that too), but textbooks rewritten, rights boldly revoked, and the most vulnerable turned into scapegoats.

It's easy to despair. It's understandable. But we are not powerless—and the principles of DEI are too important to lose without a fight.

Communities, students, workers, legislators, and organizations like American Pride Rises, which I founded, are coming together to defy these attacks and build what's next. We proudly assert that DEI is not a threat—it is a promise. We say that true patriotism demands that we fight for everyone—whether they like it or not.

This is our charge: In the face of uniformity, unfairness, and exclusion, we must promote DEI as an essential defense of democracy. In doing so, we build real opportunity into our systems, our schools, our courts, and our country. Our highest patriotism refuses to accept any less.

Democracy demands diversity, and the American dream thrives on equity and inclusion. DEI is democracy in action—with liberty and justice for all.

EMBRACE CLEAN ENERGY

BILL MCKIBBEN

SOMETIME IN THE EARLY PART OF THE 2020s we crossed an invisible line where the cost of producing energy from the sun dropped below the cost of fossil fuel. That's not yet common knowledge—we still think of photovoltaic panels and wind turbines as "alternative energy," as if they were the Whole Foods of power, nice but pricey. In fact—and more so with each passing month—they are the Costco of energy, inexpensive and available in bulk.

We live on an earth where the cheapest way to produce power is to point a sheet of glass at the sun; the second-cheapest is to let the breeze created by the sun's heating turn the blade of a wind turbine.

Beginning about the middle of 2023, we entered the really steep part of this growth curve that could redefine our future, crossing another invisible line, this one marking the installation of a gigawatt's worth of solar panels on this planet every day. (A gigawatt is about the output of a typical coal-fired power plant or nuclear reactor.) By the fall of 2024 that gigawatt was going up every eighteen hours.

We're still in the early days of this transformation—right now only about 15 percent of the planet's electricity comes from sun and wind, and only about a quarter of the energy we use comes from electricity. But exponential growth changes numbers like that very fast—in 2024, 92.5 percent of all new electricity bought online around the world came from renewables; in the US the figure was 96 percent.

By April 2025, fossil fuel was producing less than half of American electricity, for the first time ever. There's no longer a technical or financial obstacle in the way. We already have the factory capacity, mostly in China, to produce as many solar panels as the climate scientists say we need.

In May 2025 came the news that China had used five percent less coal in the first quarter of the year to produce electricity than it had in 2024—despite a surging economy, Chinese emissions were actually dropping. The suddenness of this moment is startling.

The solar cell was invented in 1954, and it took from then until 2022 to install the first terawatt worth of solar power on this planet. It took two years to get the second; the third will be quicker still. It's all brand new. But there are a few places that are running far ahead, showing what's possible. China is well on its way to being the earth's first "electro-state"; something like half of all clean energy has been installed within its borders.

And 2024 was a breakout year in California: there were finally enough solar panels that for parts of most days the state could produce from renewable sources more than 100 percent of the electricity it used; at night great batteries that had spent the afternoon soaking up sunshine often became the biggest source of supply to the electric grid of the world's fifth-largest economy.

In 2024 California used 25 percent less natural gas to produce its power than it had in 2023, which is a big number. Through mid-April 2025, as more panels and batteries came online, the numbers got even better: California was using 44 percent less natural gas to make electricity than it had just two years earlier.

On the other side of the world, in Pakistan, a flood of cheap solar panels from China let homeowners and storekeepers and factory managers build the equivalent of a third of the country's electric grid inside of a year. Peasant farmers, often just laying the panels on the ground, started pumping their irrigation water with electricity instead of generators powered with fossil fuels; diesel sales dropped 30 percent in the course of a year.

These kinds of shifts, replicated quickly in many more places, could take a real bite out of the grim predictions of climate scientists; the sun burns so we don't need to. We are in a desperate race; those scientists have told us that to stay on anything like a survivable path we must cut greenhouse gas emissions in half before the decade is out.

That target is on the bleeding edge of the technically possible, and I plan to shove us toward that deadline. I anticipate a shift that will play out over many lifetimes, and in ways that diverge dramatically from our recent history. That's because energy from the sun is not just cheap. It's also diffuse, available everywhere instead of concentrated in a few places. And that prefigures a different world with a more localized and more humane geopolitics; indeed, the sun works more reliably toward the equator, which could allow the redress of some of earth's great inequities.

In February 2025 the energy analysts at the Rocky Mountain Institute reported that renewable energy was growing twice as fast in the developing world of the Global South as in the developed world of the Global North. Relying on energy sources that are abundant instead of scarce—the sun and the wind each day produce thousands of times as much energy as we could ever use—could even reconfigure our ideas of competition and conquest. Unlike oil and gas, sun and wind can't be hoarded. If fascism scares you the way it does me, figuring out how to break the centralized power of the fossil-fuel industry is a key form of resistance.

For a species that has become almost fatally disconnected from the natural world, the sun offers a way back into a relationship with reality. We were all sun worshippers once; it's not perhaps too much to imagine that we might someday soon gaze up a little more often, maybe even breaking a little of the enchantment woven by the glowing lights in our palms. This is not, I think, a "techno-fix," but something far more fundamental.

We have the chance to join in a great global project, providing affordable energy to every human community even as we stave off our greatest threat. It could prove a unifying mission for a divided world. The last remotely comparable project was the moon shot of the 1960s, but that involved one nation putting two men on an orbiting rock. This quest involves bringing our star down to earth to make that earth work—what could be more quintessentially human?

All this hope risks sounding giddy; let my dark realism reassert itself for a moment and offer a few caveats and cautions. I'm not overly concerned about the things people usually point to. We're not going to run short of minerals to build batteries or land to put panels on. Instead, my worries stem from hard realities both physical and political.

First, this definitely comes too late to "stop global warming." We've already done fundamental damage to the planet's physical systems, to the point of altering the jet stream and weakening the Gulf Stream; we've already raced past the 1.5 degree Celsius rise in global temperature that we pledged in Paris to avoid. (In April 2025, the Trump administration fired most of the American scientists who monitor this increase, perhaps reasoning that what we don't know can't hurt us.)

Our best hope now is simply to stop the heating of the earth short of the point where it cuts civilization off at the knees, and even that will be a very close call. I have little doubt we will run the world on sun and wind forty years from now, but if it takes us anything like forty years to get there then it will be a broken planet; our energy sources will hardly matter. The march of history won't get us where we need to go fast enough; we need to force that march.

Second, there's no guarantee that the momentum of the last few years will continue. The fossil fuel industry has read the numbers too, and so they've girded for the fight. As the chairman of one big oil company said in the fall of 2024, the industry thinks we should keep burning gas and oil until "every last molecule" had been sucked from the earth. If you think that capitalism guarantees we'll pick the lowest-priced option, think again: In certain ways, solar and wind power are almost too cheap for our economy.

Investors who have gotten rich controlling the hoarded "reserves" of fossil fuel are scared of the fact that the sun delivers energy for free each time it rises above the horizon, and in their fear they're gaming our political system. The worldwide elections of 2024 saw setback after setback, with oil-soaked populists winning control in too many places.

Just as they played the game of climate denial with real success for three decades, they now engage in a kind of solutions denial, claiming we're not ready for clean energy, or offering up substitutes closer to the status quo. Some of these substitutes (geothermal power and nuclear energy, if the cost ever comes down) may offer useful side dishes to the main course of sun, wind, and batteries; others (carbon capture from power plants, biofuels) are just expensive efforts to extend the business model of this industry a little longer. All of the substitutes are effective at distracting us, especially in the distorted infosphere of greenwash and spin we inhabit.

Nowhere, of course, is that distortion more powerful than the United States, where Trump rode back into office vowing to "drill, baby, drill" and to crash the electric vehicle industry. He'd been in office four hours when he signed an order ending all federal support for wind power. (As for solar energy, the week before the election he said, "It's all steel and glass and wires. It looks like hell. And you see rabbits get caught in it.") By April, just three months into his second term, Trump was announcing plans to revive the coal industry, and his bizarre tariffs were making life harder for renewable energy developers; he cut off funding to Princeton's climate modelers on the grounds that their findings were causing "climate anxiety."

All of which is to offer a third caution: Just because the world goes in one direction, that doesn't mean every nation will follow. Yes, there's enormous momentum behind this transformation; on the last day of February 2025 the federal Energy Information Administration predicted that 93 percent of American electric generation built in Trump's first year would be carbon-free, mostly from solar.

In the first month of 2025, as Trump was taking office, sun and wind combined made up 98 percent of new generating capacity in the US. But clearly the Trump–Musk team has tried to break that momentum; already-high tariffs on Chinese solar panels have been increased again, and the administration is embarked on a sprawling effort to achieve "energy dominance" based on oil and gas.

It's an effort to stuff the solar genie back in the barrel, and we don't know yet to what degree it will succeed. The Biden administration, with the Inflation Reduction Act, set in motion transformative spending on clean energy technology, and spread the money carefully around the red states; Texas, home base of the hydrocarbon industry, is now outpacing even California in clean energy (though the state legislature, as of spring 2025, was engaged in an all-out effort to sabotage that growth).

Power from the sun can appeal to conservatives ("my home is my well-wired castle") as powerfully as it does to liberals. But the addiction to fossil fuels and all its accomplices (the giant SUV, say) runs deeper here than anyplace else; it will be a fight to turn the American page.

Much of the progress that engineers have made has come on the back of inspired activism, something we need more of. In this fight, the solar panel and the wind turbine are both the crucial machines and also the symbols of potential liberation.

And in true Hollywood fashion, our liberation and our destruction are arriving at precisely the same time, offering us a remarkable choice. Everything is going wrong, except this one big thing. Our species, at what feels like a very dark moment, can take a giant leap into the light. Of the sun.

RECOGNIZE ENTROPY

JAMES K. GALBRAITH AND JING CHEN

THE END PRODUCT OF ALL FORMS OF ACTIV-ity is waste: waste heat and chemicals, including and especially carbon dioxide. In the past century, the increasing concentration of carbon dioxide in the atmosphere has been linked to increased global temperatures. This is the climate crisis of which many scientists have warned, which the world's governments are now struggling to contain.

How do these matters look from our perspective of

thermodynamic law and entropy economics? The study of past data and our long-term experience show that the increase of carbon dioxide in the atmosphere is highly beneficial to living organisms in general—and to human civilizations. However, changes do not benefit everyone. Global warming will not benefit everyone. To be a bit glib, it may well be much better for plants and microbes than it is for humans. That is because carbon dioxide is a waste product for industrial civilizations, but it is a raw material, or resource, for other forms of life.

The end of the most recent ice age about ten thousand years ago was a global warming. It generated great floods in many places. The Bible recorded the story of Noah, a story of global warming and a great flood. Noah (if he existed) lived in a time of global warming. Warming generates a huge melting of ice. Warming generates huge amounts of rain. Warming generates floods. At the time of Noah, floods did devour some low-lying areas. (Among other things, the melting of the ice sheet covering much of North America carved out the St. Lawrence River.) But the warming ended the ice age. The warming energized the globe and greatly increased the carrying capacity of earth.

After Noah, the earth greened, and human civilizations flourished.

We can expect some of this process to be repeated as the earth warms more. Evaporation and rain should increase. More fresh water, along with more carbon dioxide, should feed the plant life of the planet. More plants should mean better soil, and more food from the natural processes of biological reproduction and growth. What then is the problem? The problem is that this will take a very long time. And meanwhile, the present world has been built on other lines. We have made fixed investments that changing circumstances will render unprofitable on a massive scale.

It is obvious that the current structure of human civilization is not well adapted to the coming world. It is not just that we are accustomed to certain temperature ranges in certain places. Among other things, we have built our population on our food supply. We have built our food supply on fossil fuels, which are becoming scarce and expensive, and the benefits of climate change for agriculture—if they arrive—will arrive slowly and will not fully replace the low-entropy sources on which we now depend. Climate change, together with resource depletion, portends a food crisis.

In 1930, the human population of the entire world was just two billion. Today it is around eight billion and rising toward ten billion. This vast increase in carrying capacity, at unprecedented levels of prosperity in many countries, is due to the use of high-quality resources: oil, gas, and nuclear energy in addition to coal (which dates from the eighteenth century), as well as minerals and other components of chemical fertilizers. The warm, wet earth to come will be a greener place. But it will not be green enough, or biologically rich enough, to support the food we presently need for the population we currently have.

Quite likely, as high-quality fossil fuel resources are depleted, the industrial basis of food production will decline long before the richer foundations of new plant life are present. The competition for food is existential for human populations. If the food supply falters, the world's population will fall, in a general biological depression. And not only that. It is also that we have built major cities by the seaside. We have a vast fixed investment in global trade at existing ports.

We have calculated the effect of floods and storms and sea-level rise, as well as riverine floods, and the melting of glaciers in the Himalaya and elsewhere, on our constructions. We've assumed supplies of fresh water for our farms and cities. We've built our health systems to treat chronic rather than infectious diseases. And we've calculated wrongly.

These are among the problems that climate change poses for humans. Can climate change be stopped? Like everyone else, we would like to think so. But so far, the evidence as we see it suggests otherwise. We have not slowed the use of fossil fuels or the increase in CO_2 emissions. Even the large investments underway in renewable energy sources—in harvesting sunlight directly—are both intensive in their own use of fossil fuels and serve as an addition to, not a replacement for, the consumption of fossil fuels in their present ordinary uses. This is just as William Stanley Jevons predicted a century and a half ago. For this reason, we are not optimistic.

As the climate warms, sea-level rise could be as much as ten meters. That much could take centuries, if it ever happens. But with just a few meters of rise, along with other changes such as shifts in ocean currents in the Atlantic, quite a bit of what we have built will be destroyed, and much more will become unprofitable to operate. London, New York, and Shanghai are among the most threatened, and wealthiest, places.

Further, the rising cost of fossil fuels will destroy the profitability of many existing industries, especially in transportation, on which trade and commerce depend. Uncertainty and fear will discourage further fixed investments. Existing supply chains will break down, and integrated global industries will shrink or collapse. Mitigation and adaptation to climate change will take second place to the requirements of survival, if there are not enough resources for both.

In short, we have a gigantic backlog of fixed investments that are likely to become increasingly hard to maintain and unprofitable to operate. Retreat and rebuilding will occur, but these cost resources, require planning and organization, and are unlikely to be carried out at the same standard as in the past.

Indeed, our civilization, the fossil fuel civilization, is in difficulty and will get into more difficulty as the costs of extracting and transporting fossil fuels rise and as the existing infrastructure ages. This difficulty is not caused by the increase in carbon dioxide in the atmosphere. But it will make dealing with climate change more challenging.

There is yet another grave difficulty ahead: the biological depression that is already underway. In every high-income country, and most of the developing world as well, fertility rates have fallen below replacement levels. This process has been going on for at least fifty years. In extreme cases, such as Japan, China, and some countries in Europe, population will likely decline quite rapidly as the present century unfolds. In others, notably the US, immigration will mitigate the loss of fertility—but only for a time.

The decline in individual fertility rates means that overall human population growth will slow, stop, and eventually start falling. Why is that? Human reproduction rates are a personal decision. And in overwhelming numbers, those making the decisions are opting to have fewer children. The most likely explanation, in our view, is economic. In wealthy countries, children are expensive—in economic terms they are a fixed cost—and they reduce the income and wealth opportunities available to young adults. A rising cost of resources, on top of this, simply means that the free resources available to families decline, and with them the margin of maneuver that makes having children attractive.

Austerity and precarity compound these problems. The billions of micro decisions that underlie population growth have macro consequences. With fewer children, human populations age. The burden of caring for the elderly increases. Investments tend to go to meet that challenge, rather than toward easing the cost of having children. As women age, birth cohorts decline, so the number of potential parents further limits the number of potential children. A decline in population begets a further decline. There is little basis for optimism that this process can or will be reversed, even when populations are much smaller, in a few centuries, than they are today.

Human society has become complex, rigid, and fragile. Whether present human society can withstand even relatively small changes in the operating conditions laid down by previous human societies under the earlier conditions is an open question. The change from coal to oil helped precipitate the Great Depression. The phenomenon we may be facing is similar, but on a much larger and more serious scale, over a longer time, and without an early off-ramp toward renewed prosperity. Although life will continue to prosper on our planet, existing civilizations and especially some of their wealthier elements will tend to crumble away.

It seems likely that, in the distant future, most humans will live in tropical and subtropical conditions, with far fewer amenities and comforts than we enjoy today. And with the intervening decline of fertility and populations, fewer humans will inhabit this warmed-up earth. They will, most probably, look back on our civilizations with curiosity and, perhaps, regret.

Our society is not supported by the stock market. Our society is supported by food, electricity, and fuels. Our society is supported by grocery stores, cashiers and stockers, farmers, truck drivers, and factory workers. This becomes plain and simple during a crisis. We need more people, more young people with strong immune systems, more young people who can work effectively under stress.

To achieve a younger population, we can't keep our eyes glued to the financial indicators or to such measures as gross domestic product, conceived in another age for an entirely different purpose. We should pay attention to birthrates, to public health, to the cost and quality of education, and to other vital biophysical indicators. This is the first step we need to take. We may not succeed in any event, but this is what we should do. It will be the next generations, not the present ones, that will have to cope with the world to come.

Because of the importance of energy in our lives, people have pursued the dream of convenient and cheap renewable energy since time immemorial. In the course of history, many people have believed they discovered an inexhaustible source of energy or invented one or another kind of perpetual motion machine. They think their discoveries or inventions could be put to practical use in large scale once necessary technical improvements can be made. However, more rigorous investigation led to the development of thermodynamic theory, which rules out the possibility of a perpetual, or renewable, energy source without external input.

This helps us envision the future of human society in an environment of increasingly scarce and costly natural resources. The main results can be summarized as follows:

• The survival and prosperity of human society depends entirely on the availability of natural resources.

- Although the forms of natural resources are diverse, they can be understood from the unifying principle as low-entropy sources.
- To use natural resources, fixed structures are required, which themselves consume resources.
- When certain structures can generate positive returns on the use of natural resources over an indefinite period, these structures are called living organisms.
- It is the unique chemical property of carbon that enables it to become the backbone of life. The major nonrenewable energy resources that our industrial civilization builds on—such as coal, oil, and natural gas—are generated from the remains of the living organisms. They all contain carbon.
- Our industrial civilization is bringing on a combination of increased high-quality resource costs, a warming climate, rising sea level, and declining human fertility.

A warmer climate will, very likely, green the earth. But the other factors will make much of our current civilization obsolete and much of our economic activity unprofitable.

The future of human society is likely, for a long time, to devolve back to smaller populations, shorter life spans, higher variable costs, and lower fixed costs, along with smaller countries and harsher inequalities both within and between them.

Social arrangements, advance planning, new energy sources, and new investments can mitigate the suffering from this transition, up to a point. But this, quite likely so far as we understand it, is the biophysical reality with which future economists, engineers, and planners will have to engage.

RESIST MEDIA CONSOLIDATION

CORPORATE MEDIA CONSOLIDATION PUTS HOLLYWOOD, AND DEMOCRACY, AT RISK

JANE FONDA

AS I WRITE THIS, THE FUTURE OF THE entertainment industry is being negotiated behind closed doors.

Warner Bros. Discovery is preparing for its sale, and every artist I know—from actors to writers to journalists—is glued to the trades, whispering in hallways, wondering: Which company will buy WBD? Netflix? Paramount

Skydance? Comcast NBCUniversal? A sovereign wealth fund from the Middle East? Something else entirely? And what will it mean for all of us?

We don't know which company Warner Bros. Discovery will choose as its new owner. We don't know what price will be paid or who will be left standing afterward. But we don't need to know the final outcome to understand the danger. The threat of this merger in any form is an alarming escalation in a consolidation crisis that threatens the entire entertainment industry, the public it serves, and—potentially—the First Amendment itself.

Regardless of which company ends up acquiring Warner Bros. Discovery or its parts, the resulting impact is clear: consolidation at this scale would be catastrophic for an industry built on free expression, for the creative workers who power it, and for consumers who depend on a free, independent media ecosystem to understand the world. It will mean fewer jobs, fewer opportunities to sell work, fewer creative risks, fewer news sources, and far less diversity in the stories Americans get to hear.

For actors, writers, directors, editors, designers,

animators, and crew already fighting for work, consolidation will lessen the overall demand for their skills. And when only a handful of mega-companies control the entire pipeline, they gain the power to steamroll every guild—SAG-AFTRA, the WGA, the PGA, the DGA, IATSE, everyone—making it harder for workers to bargain, harder to stand up for themselves, and harder to make a living at all.

But as dangerous as the economic fallout could be, it is not what scares me most. What terrifies me—and should terrify anyone who cares about a free society—is how this administration has used anticipated mergers as tools of political pressure and censorship.

We've already seen this at work. During the Skydance-Paramount merger proceedings, the chairman of the FCC launched an investigation into *60 Minutes* over routine editing of an interview with then-Vice President Kamala Harris—a move his own predecessor said was "fundamentally at odds with the First Amendment." Paramount then paid the sitting president $16 million to settle a lawsuit widely considered meritless; installed a former administration ambassador as a "bias monitor" overseeing editorial content at CBS; and eliminated all diversity, equity and inclusion programs. Shortly after Stephen Colbert criticized the company's political capitulation, he was fired. Then came nearly 2,000 layoffs across the company and the elimination of CBS' Race and Culture Unit.

This is not how media companies behave in a healthy democracy. It's what political leverage over media companies looks like, and it's right out of the authoritarian playbook. We saw the pattern repeat with Nexstar, which is pursuing an acquisition of Tegna. After the FCC Chairman publicly attacked Jimmy Kimmel, Nexstar—which will require support from the FCC to complete its transaction—became the first broadcaster to pull Kimmel's show from its ABC affiliate stations. Again, this is not a coincidence. It's bootlicking.

I want to be very clear: The First Amendment is not partisan, and neither is standing up to defend it. Even conservative leaders have warned that the administration is operating outside legal and ethical bounds. When the FCC Chair threatened Kimmel, several prominent Trump allies objected. Senator Ted Cruz said that using merger reviews to pressure media companies "creates a dangerous precedent"—one that could just as easily be used to silence conservatives under a future Democratic administration. "They will silence us," he warned. He was right to be concerned. Everyone should be. Without the foundation of the First Amendment, every other aspect of our democratic society, including the American guarantee that we are free to live as we choose, is at risk.

I know that members of our industry are terrified to speak up because it could entail criticizing the very companies their livelihoods depend on or might depend on in the future. And all of this is unfolding at a moment when our industry is already on its knees: recovering from historic strikes, wildfires that shut down productions, and relentless layoffs and bracing for the effects of AI advancement. Opportunities are evaporating. Middle-class careers are disappearing. People are fighting for scraps.

The stakes are high. But when we stand together, we are powerful. We can insist—together—that the First Amendment is not a bargaining chip to be traded away during a merger review process or meritless lawsuit negotiations. And we must demand that the Justice Department and state attorneys general evaluate every proposed entertainment merger for compliance with antitrust laws. These reviews cannot be treated as procedural formalities or political leverage; they are the last line of defense against media consolidation that threatens competition, creative freedom, and democratic discourse.

My father, Henry Fonda, and others built the Committee for the First Amendment when artists were being jailed, blacklisted and silenced during the Red Scare. They understood that the only antidote to fear is solidarity. We recently relaunched the Committee, which now has over 2,000 members across the entertainment industry, because the only way to fight back is collectively.

And if we don't speak now, we may have no industry—and no democracy—left to defend. We don't yet know which company will buy Warner Bros. Discovery. But we do know what's at stake: our jobs, our creative freedom and the constitutional promise that every American has the right to speak, report, criticize, satirize, investigate and imagine without fear.

This is not a partisan fight. It is a fight for our creativity, our livelihoods and our most fundamental rights as Americans.

I choose to stand up. I hope you will join me.

DITCH NEOLIBERALISM

JOSEPH E. STIGLITZ

I HOPE THIS IS THE MOMENT IN HISTORY IN which neoliberalism's failures are so apparent that it will be abandoned. Gabriel Boric, who became Chile's president in 2022, captured the spirit of the moment on the eve of his primary victory when he said, "If Chile was the birthplace of neoliberalism, it will also be its grave!"

I want to discuss an alternative framework, progressive capitalism (or a rejuvenated social democracy), which puts the well-being of all citizens at its center and goes beyond material goods to incorporate a sense of security and freedom.

It takes human flourishing as the objective of our economic and social system, which includes citizens leading meaningful and creative lives. Good health, education, and a certain level of material well-being and security are necessary but not sufficient for this. We sometimes forget, but the economy is supposed to serve society, not the other way around.

I've emphasized how all the rules and regulations, laws and programs, shape the economy and society. I will center my discussion of progressive capitalism around eight themes.

CREATING A LEARNING SOCIETY

The world is ever-changing, and it changes in ways that are unpredictable. This view is markedly different from the equilibrium theory that was so influential in the early years of economics and continues to be today. We need to see institutions and governance structures through evolutionary lenses, where change and learning are always occurring.

Our technology is changing. Our tastes are changing. Our understanding of our social and economic systems is changing. And our understanding of the physical world around us is changing. Indeed, one of the important sources of change in our economy and society is from learning—not just from the discoveries of new technologies through advances of science but also from learning more about how our complex political/economic/social system works.

As social scientists, we want to understand the determinants and directions of change; as policymakers and citizens, we want to direct the change while knowing that we never have full control. At best, we may be able to nudge the economy and society one way or another.

Learning is not simply getting a formal education; it occurs throughout life. But there is also institutional learning, where we learn how to redesign institutional arrangements to make them better at achieving the objectives for which they are created and more adept at coordinating with other institutions.

We can learn how to design institutions to transform themselves from within and respond to the ever-changing environments in which they function. Of course, typically there is some learning, but not as much as there could be. Central bankers did a better job in 2008 than they did in the Great Depression partly because they learned from the failures of that earlier episode. But it was evident in the run-up to the Great Recession that even economists like Federal Reserve chair Ben Bernanke, who claimed to have learned the lessons of the Great Depression, really hadn't. Bernanke supported Alan Greenspan (who preceded him as chair) and most other members of the Fed as they pushed the deregulation that led to the Great Recession. One of the main lessons of the Great Depression was that under-regulated financial markets are dangerous.

In recent years, the US has embraced industrial policies in an attempt to shape the direction of the economy. It now recognizes that markets on their own won't suffice. The US government has also pushed a green economy, supported the development of Covid-19 vaccines, and recognized the country's excessive dependence on chips made abroad. Inevitably, because the US hasn't done much of this type of policy before (outside the military), there will be much to learn. Mistakes will be made.

But the discovery of a mistake is no more reason to abandon such policies than recognizing that the Fed's failure in the Great Depression and Great Recession is a reason to shut down the Fed. For instance, when the US government lent a half-billion dollars to Elon Musk for Tesla in 2009, it successfully supported the advancement of electric vehicle technology.

But it made a mistake. It failed to insist on a share of the upside potential, which it easily could have done by insisting on receiving shares, for instance. If it had, the government (and American taxpayers) would have more than made up for the losses incurred in other technology loans and investments. It will capture some of the profits through taxes on individual income and corporate profits, but far less than if it had included the profit-sharing provision in the contract. The lesson to be learned is that it's important to pick projects well, but it's also important to design contracts well.

A learning society, then, entails both individual and institutional learning—and this learning is indeed part of human flourishing, a basic objective of a good society. Learning is a never-ending process.

I have contrasted the equilibrium perspective of standard (neoliberal) economics—its assumption of a harmonious world in equilibrium without change—with the ever-changing world we live in often marked by intense conflict. We are finally beginning to understand that we are crashing headlong into our planetary boundaries. We must adapt. We have no choice. But the best way forward is almost never obvious. Thus, we take an evolutionary perspective with a focus on adaptation rather than on equilibrium. Progressive capitalism, I believe, will facilitate the evolution of our economy in ways that will help create a good society.

A DECENTRALIZED ECONOMY WITH A RICH ECOLOGY OF INSTITUTIONS

Our economic system has to be decentralized, with a multiplicity of economic units—many enterprises and other entities (of different kinds) making decisions about what to do and how to do it. The world is too complex to be centrally planned, as communism called for more than a hundred years ago.

Having many units generates more learning about their own capabilities, about technology, about what others want. Each unit experiments, with different units having different conceptions about appropriate objectives and how to achieve them.

In recent years, much of the debate has been over the relative roles played by public (government) institutions versus private (for-profit) companies. This perspective unnecessarily narrows the discussion. Any well-functioning economy or society requires a mix of types of institutions, not only public and private for-profit, but also cooperatives, private not-for-profit, and so on.

The governmental institutions need to operate at multiple levels, including local, state or provincial, national, and global. These institutions need to exert checks and balances on one another, and the overall governance structures must limit power and its abuse.

I want to emphasize that there must be large parts of the economy that are not and cannot be driven by profit.

These include much of the health, education, and care sectors, in which the narrow pursuit of profit often leads to perverse results. The private prison system has failed its core mission of rehabilitating prisoners.

In the US, the most successful institutions that explain a lot of the country's overall achievements are its great research universities, which are either foundations, like Harvard and Columbia, or public. In other countries, too, the best universities are not-for-profit foundations, like Oxford and Cambridge, or state institutions, like the grandes écoles and the Sorbonne in France. Likewise, the cooperative part of the US financial system (typically referred to as credit unions) was the only segment that, for the most part, behaved in a socially responsible way both before and after the 2008 financial crisis.

But even profit-making firms would be different under progressive capitalism than under neoliberalism. Their ethos would be different from our current firms hell-bent on maximizing shareholder wealth, whatever the cost to the rest of our society. These private, profit-making firms wouldn't be revered as they are today. They have no magic potion that allows them to solve problems that others can't; it's just that some problems can be better solved by profit-maximizing firms and others by other kinds of entities.

POWER, THE COMPETITIVE PARADIGM, AND PROGRESSIVE CAPITALISM

Modern economics begins with a model of perfect competition, in which the economy is in a harmonious equilibrium. Competition policy isn't even required, because the economy will naturally be competitive.

Here, the neoliberals depart markedly from Adam Smith. Elsewhere, I have noted Smith's concern about the proclivity of businesspeople to collude against the public interest. Conservative devotees of Smith champion him only to the extent that he agrees with their views. The fact is, the economy is not naturally competitive, in the narrow sense economists use that term.

For economists, a truly competitive economy is one in which no firm has the power to raise prices, impose contractual terms on others, or block the entry of firms so that profits won't be bid away. We've already seen these conditions aren't true in today's world—from the unsavory nondisclosure agreements and compulsory arbitrary provisions, to the persistent profits that are most visible in the digital giants.

Progressive capitalism recognizes that power exists, and that the distribution of power is a central concern; limiting power is crucial. There are power relations within and between the entities that constitute our economy and their interactions with citizens, and some can and do take advantage of others.

Power relations are central to understanding economics, politics, and society. America's economy was built on enslaved labor, hardly the manifestation of a free market. The country's legal structure was designed to enforce slavery and preserve the power relationship.

Power relations are central to understanding the growing inequality and widespread perception that the system is rigged, which have played such an important role in the disillusionment with democracy and its institutions and the growth of populism.

Progressive capitalism would achieve a better balance by restraining corporate power, encouraging entry of new firms (by increasing the availability of finance and technology for entrants), and strengthening workers' rights, including through encouraging unionization.

GOVERNANCE

The term *governance* refers to the rules that determine who makes what decisions and what the objectives are. Corporate governance relates to the rules affecting companies' decisions. Firm managers have enormous power in all the decisions of the company—how it treats workers, customers, shareholders, and stakeholders. Corporate governance laws specify and limit these powers.

Milton Friedman put forward an idea that became a central tenet of twentieth-century neoliberal capitalism, enshrined in the laws of many states: shareholder capitalism. The only goal for managers of firms is to maximize shareholder value. There's no responsibility to pay attention to workers, customers, the community, or even the environment, except to the extent that their actions, with respect to those "stakeholders," affect share prices.

On the face of it, there was something noxious about this doctrine. It put Gordon Gekko, the fictional character in the movie *Wall Street*, and his ethos that "greed is good," on a pedestal. Adam Smith may have suggested that the pursuit of self-interest led to the well-being of society, but he rushed to qualify that statement. Not so Friedman.

Even as Friedman enunciated that doctrine in a famous article in the *New York Times* in 1970, economist Sandy Grossman and I, along with others, were analyzing the conditions under which shareholder maximization would lead to societal well-being. We showed that those conditions were extraordinarily restrictive and not satisfied by any real economy. But our articles, published in journals like the *Quarterly Journal of Economics* and the *Journal of Finance*, were far less influential than Friedman's. He was an apostle of the free market and possessed enormous persuasive abilities, putting forward arguments that people like Ronald Reagan and Margaret Thatcher wanted to hear. He was less concerned about whether there were analytics behind these arguments. Shareholder capitalism may have succeeded in enriching the owners of firms, but it didn't lead to shared societal prosperity.

REBALANCING POWER RELATIONS

Rebalancing power relationships in every aspect of our society (the household, the firm, the economy, politics) is essential for shared prosperity and creating a good and decent society. Today's imbalance of power has expanded the freedom of big corporations even as it constrained the freedom of ordinary citizens. People feel it intensely in the frustrations of day-to-day life. There is no real consumer choice and each company is as exploitive as the next, with awful provisions like mandatory arbitration of disputes and usurious fees. On top of that, there are often two-hour waits to talk to a "service" representative.

The Supreme Court has weighed in to tilt the balance even more in favor of expanding the freedom and power of big business at everyone else's expense, ruling out class-action lawsuits in the context of the arbitrations that people have effectively been forced to agree to. This might seem like a small matter, but power relations are created within a system rule by rule, case by case. So today, to achieve a better balance—to replace neoliberal capitalism with progressive capitalism—we have to reconstruct our economic and legal system, rule by rule, regulation by regulation, institution by institution.

ORGANIZING SOCIETY

There are multiple ways to organize society. Some arrangements give more power to some groups, less to others; some benefit one group at the expense of others. Traditionally, the rules are set by the powerful for the benefit of the powerful. That should be unacceptable. No real democracy would allow it.

There is an alternative basis for adjudicating among possible arrangements, an application of established philosophical principles underlying what social justice means and what a socially just and fair economic, political, and social system would look like—what would be chosen behind a veil of ignorance.

It may be hard to put ourselves into such a mindset and to think through the implications; there may even be dilemmas and quandaries in doing so. And when we complete our exercise, we still may not reach unanimity, or even consensus. But I suspect that the gulf in views we see today would be narrowed. It is possible to make compromises to enable us to move forward in the quest for a good and just society.

CHECKS AND BALANCES

One of the arguments for the decentralized economic structures described above, with their rich ecologies of institutional arrangements, is the potential that such diversity has for exercising checks and balances. Civil society and the press provide a check against each other and against for-profit entities and the government.

In political science, the standard argument for the division of powers within government relates to checks and balances; but equally important, we need checks and balances within society. Indeed, whatever the formal structures, if there is excessive power in the for-profit, private sector, the rich and powerful firms will exercise undue influence in the public sphere.

ECONOMIC DIVIDES, POWER, AND SOCIAL JUSTICE

Checks and balances won't work if there is an excess concentration of wealth and income in society. If we are to develop a system that works for the common good, an essential ingredient in any system claiming to be a good society, we have to have greater equality in all its dimensions, especially equality of opportunity.

This does not mean the elimination of all economic inequality—a system that achieved this would enervate incentives, and even a touch of realism involves recognizing that material incentives will be important for large fractions of the population.

Particularly problematic is the growing power imbalance, increasing concentrations of wealth and corporate power mirrored by the evisceration of the power and incomes of workers. A social justice agenda is an important part of progressive capitalism. It attempts to reduce levels of inequalities, and not just in income and wealth. It's especially attentive to inequalities that arise from various forms of exploitation.

Access to basic health care is an important part of social justice, and should be a human right (as it is in the Universal Declaration of Human Rights adopted in 1948). Progressive capitalism recognizes this, and most advanced countries have figured out that the fairest and more efficient way to provide health care is some form of public provision, sometimes supplemented by private provision, especially in any country with a high level of income and wealth inequality. Many people in the US, however, seem to find this hard to accept.

The current system, even after the passage of the Affordable Care Act, has left many without adequate health care or no real choice of provider, the opposite of the law's intention. That's why in the US a public option—in which government is one of the providers people can choose—is so important. It enhances choice and competition, which is another way to limit the exploitation by market actors.

CREATE A HEALTHY ECONOMY

HAROLD MEYERSON

IN 2021, HISTORIAN GABRIEL WINANT AU-thored a remarkable book, *The Next Shift: The Fall of Industry and the Rise of Health Care in Rust Belt America*, that told the story of both 20th-century Pittsburgh and the transformation of the American workforce. Its focus was the decline of the steel industry, which had dominated the Pittsburgh economy, and the rise of the health-care industry, which came to dominate that same economy as steelworkers either aged out of their jobs or saw those jobs eliminated, in both cases saddled with industry-related infirmities that required medical care. Its focus was also the challenge to the Pittsburgh economy as the number of steelworkers dwindled (their union had made them among the best-paid blue-collar workers in America), and the number of health care workers rose (whose wages weren't comparable to the steelworkers', though the subsequent unionization of a number of them only partly diminished that gap).

I was reminded of Winant's book by recent reports from the Bureau of Labor Statistics, which documented the declining number of workers in virtually every sector of the economy over the past 13 months, save only health care. During 2025, the number of workers employed in the manufacturing, construction, and retail sectors dropped by 115,000. The health-care industry, by contrast, added 437,000 net new workers, while the social assistance sector, which consists chiefly of home health care aides, grew by 321,000.

The overall private-sector economy grew by just

181,000 jobs in 2025, which means that it would have ended up with 577,000 fewer jobs on December 31 than it had on the previous January 1, had health care and social assistance not boosted it into positive numbers.

These trends have continued into this year. The BLS report for January 2026 shows that nearly all the jobs created last month were in health care and social assistance. Jobs in construction also increased, but that was largely attributable to the boom in data centers. The number of jobs in residential construction continued to shrink.

Donald Trump deserves to take his lumps for part of the overall job destruction, most particularly by downsizing the number of federal government employees and impeding private-sector expansion by inflicting tariffs on imports that employers needed to manufacture their products or sell to consumers. But these larger trends predate Trump's second term and signal more profound and long-lasting challenges for the American economy.

Even before AI became sufficiently advanced to (apparently) supplant thousands of workers in the tech industry, programmable machine tools had long been replacing workers on assembly lines. Fifteen years ago, the then-CEO of U.S. Steel told me that two workers were then turning out the same level of product that had required ten workers just one decade earlier. A rolling mill today has hardly any workers on the shop floor; rather, the remaining workers are in booths suspended on catwalks above the floor, regulating the flow of molten ingots by monitoring screens and turning dials and switches.

The offshoring of factories, call centers, and any facility where the work comes cheaper abroad has been common practice for financialized American corporations for the past 45 years. Even more fundamentally, those corporations have greatly reduced the share of their operating income going to their internal investment (new or improved facilities, research and development) while raising the share going to shareholders.

In the decades preceding 2000, approximately 4.8 percent of U.S. corporations' operating income went to share buybacks; that share rose to *21.2 percent* in the decades following. Rewarding owners, in other words, took precedence over producing products and creating jobs. The meta goal of American capitalism, however unstated it may have been, was to create the K-shaped economy we have today.

But American consumers have one demand that can't be denied: health care. And as the number of elderly Americans has grown, so has that demand. As is not the case for other sectors of the economy, demand for health care is neither countercyclical nor pro-cyclical; it's not cyclical at all. Despite the fact that ours is the only nation with an advanced economy in which health care is not universal, despite the fact that our distinct version of health care costs far more than that of any other nation, despite the cutbacks to health coverage that Trump demanded in order to cut taxes on the rich, the sector continues to grow. Were that to stop, the entire economy would stagnate (at best), or plunge into recession.

There's no single panacea that can turn around the shrinking job numbers in the rest of the economy. Technology, of which AI is merely the tip of the spear, will continue to replace humans, and the fact that fewer than six percent of private-sector American workers are unionized means that 94 percent of them won't even have a vehicle with which to resist such wholesale replacements.

Some regulation of AI will be enacted (let's hope) to protect its consumers; protecting human workers is clearly also needed, but likely more difficult to achieve. The kind of industrial policy that the Biden administration began is also necessary, though 21st-century factories will require a small fraction of the workers needed to turn out products that used to require hundreds or thousands.

Growing government investment in infrastructure and education remains the surest bet to boost underperforming sectors of the economy. When it comes to private-sector investment practices, jump-starting a return to internal investment on the part of American corporations will require nationwide laws and regulations effectively mandating definancialization—banning share buybacks; raising taxes on investment income, top-executive pay, and excessive (i.e., socially dysfunctional and politically destabilizing) wealth to the levels required to definancialize our economy.

No easy lifts there, though all polling shows that taxing the very rich is very popular. And as job creation outside health care continues to stagnate, raising government investment in ways that create jobs may well surmount the ideological hurdles it often confronts.

REDISTRIBUTE

BROOK NO SHIT

CORY DOCTOROW

WILLIAM GIBSON FAMOUSLY SAID, "THE future is here. It's just not evenly distributed." This is usually interpreted to mean that sharp-eyed observers can find little bits and bobs of gleaming new technology seeded around their surroundings, like a kid on a solar-charged e-bike bombing down a gravel road with a cargo box full of vaccines in a region where no one has running water or grid electricity.

But I know Bill, and there's no way that his unevenly distributed futures are exclusively utopian. Gibson is a man who is uniquely and brilliantly attuned to all the ways that technology can go horribly, lavishly wrong.

Here's how I think the future's uneven distribution goes: All the worst technologies appear first among the least socially powerful among us, and then work their way up the privilege gradient until we're all struggling under them.

I call this the "shitty technology adoption curve." If you're a bright tech entrepreneur with a terrible idea that will make people's lives miserable, you can't just inflict it on someone like me, a middle-aged, middle-class mouthy white guy. I'll scream bloody murder.

So you start with prisoners. Asylum seekers. People in mental institutions. Parolees. Then it's school kids, people on welfare, gig workers. Then it's college kids, interns, Medicare recipients, blue-collar workers, bottom-rung white-collar workers. At each stage, all the rough edges of the terrible new technology are sanded down on the bodies of its victims, and the depredations that can't be softened are instead normalized, one group at a time.

Eventually, the shitty technology comes for us all, working its way past middle-class writers and white-collar workers, all the way up to the C-suite. Twenty years ago, if you found yourself eating your meals under the unblinking eye of a CCTV camera, it was because you were an inmate at a Supermax prison. Today, all it signifies is that you were unwise enough to buy a "smart" home camera from Apple, Google, or (God help you) Facebook.

Tech workers enjoyed decades of absolutely top-tier workplace conditions. A tech industry "campus" had many perks: free gourmet meals, day-care facilities, gyms, laundry services—all the mom-for-hire comforts that were lampooned in shows like *Silicon Valley*. Tech bosses didn't lavish these extras on tech workers out of affection: it came out of a cold-blooded calculation that tech workers were hard to replace, and in enormous demand, so they had to be kept happy or they might defect to a rival.

But tech workers aren't the only workers tech bosses employ—indeed, they represent a tiny slice of a typical tech business. From Amazon's warehouse workers and delivery drivers to Facebook's overseas content moderators to Apple's Chinese factory workers, the largest tech workforce labors under some of the worst conditions of any workers in any sector.

Amazon's warehouses have the highest rate of on-the-job injuries—including serious injuries, even maimings—of its industry. Amazon drivers are put on quotas so punishing that they piss in bottles and defecate in bags. Their eyes and mouths are constantly monitored by "AI" cameras, and they are disciplined for not looking where the camera thinks they should be, or for singing along to the radio ("distracted driving").

The reason Jeff Bezos and Andy Jassy treat Amazon coders well and treat Amazon drivers and packers horribly is not that they are sentimentally attached to the one group and contemptuous of the other. The reason Amazon coders get to show up for work with pink mohawks, facial piercings, and black T-shirts with weird slogans their bosses don't understand is that their bosses are afraid of them.

The future of those coders is here; it's just not evenly distributed yet. If you want to know how Amazon will treat its coders once they can be readily replaced, just look at Amazon warehouse workers and drivers. They're the early adopters of Amazon's preferred labor conditions. There's no reason coders can't piss in bottles.

For a man with a dick-shaped rocket, Jeff Bezos sure has an abiding hatred of our kidneys.

Apple chief executive officer Tim Cook has a reputation for being a kind of cuddly tech boss who stands out from the pack. But the reason Apple's board picked Cook to replace cofounder Steve Jobs after he juice-cleansed his way into an early cancer death wasn't Cook's sunny disposition.

Cook's signature achievement prior to his elevation to CEO, the deed that led to his accumulation of more than $2 billion in personal wealth, was figuring out how to offshore Apple's production to factories in China. This involved establishing labor oversight and discipline in those remote Chinese factories that was so overwhelming and brutal that Foxconn, Apple's primary contractor, had to install suicide nets around the factories in "iPhone City" to catch workers who leaped to their deaths rather than face another day on the job.

We don't have to speculate about how Tim Cook treats workers he's not afraid of. The suicide nets have settled the matter. This is what Apple's tech workers can look forward to, once Tim Cook is no longer worried about replacing them.

The bad news is that tech has resolved its labor scarcity problem. As I noted earlier, the US tech sector fired 260,000 workers in 2023. In the first half of 2024, another 100,000 tech workers joined their unemployed colleagues on the breadline.

The scarcity that was at the root of tech workers' power has ended, and their power has evaporated. Scarcity-based labor power is always temporary, and bosses do everything they can to hasten its end, from demanding a halt to Covid relief checks in a bid to force more workers into the labor market, to hiring undocumented immigrants or children, to offshoring.

Throughout labor history, there's only ever been one mechanism that working people could use to protect their pay and working conditions, through times of labor scarcity and labor supply: unions.

Unionization has been in retreat for forty years—the same period during which antitrust law was in its induced coma. The same people who killed antitrust also killed unions: the neoliberal economists who have served as court sorcerers to presidents—Republican and Democrat—since Reagan.

And just as antitrust is enjoying a global revival, so, too, are unions. The favorability numbers for unions among Americans have attained heights not seen in generations, and more American workers than ever want to join unions.

Paradoxically, union membership is still falling. That's down to bad union leaders—the kinds of union leaders you'd expect to find occupying leadership roles after decades of union collapse. These are the union bosses who signed off on "two-tier" contracts that reserved union benefits for the most senior workers in the shop, while still requiring new hires to pay dues to a union that negotiated contracts that denied those workers any protections.

If you wanted to design a union contract that systematically destroys solidarity among workers, you couldn't do any better than this. American unions have bank balances that are at historic peaks, but they spend less on union organizing every year. This must change.

America's biggest unions squandered a historic opportunity under Joe Biden, whose National Labor Relations

Board was more sympathetic to workers than any NLRB since the New Deal. The fact that American labor entered the second set of Trump years with fewer unionized workers than existed at the start of the Biden years is grotesque. The labor leaders who sat out a once-in-a-generation opportunity to unionize millions of Americans begging to join up are worse than useless. We need to occupy our unions and get rid of these bastards.

That's happening. A little. Since the Covid pandemic, some of America's biggest, most corrupt, most stagnant unions have held their first free and fair leadership elections in living memory. The most notable success story here is the UAW, which, as its website notes, is "one of the largest and most diverse unions in North America." No longer just an autoworkers' union, the organization has members in a broad array of economic sectors.

The story of how the UAW finally threw out its corrupt, barnacle-suctioned old guard and elevated the firebrand Shawn Fain to its presidency in 2023 is instructive. UAW reformers helped organize an unlikely shop: Harvard's grad students, who struggle to survive in a precarious and brutal workplace, with an employer sitting on untold billions. (Not for nothing is Harvard referred to as "a hedge fund with an inconvenient university attached to it.") The newly unionized Harvard kids memorized the entire UAW rulebook, analyzing it and planning strategy.

At the leadership conference in 2023, these new UAW members served as a defensive line for the reformers. Every time the old guard tried a parliamentary trick to either call or delay a vote, or shut down a meeting or a line of questioning, one of these Harvard kids would pop up from the audience to give a chapter-and-verse explanation of why the move was illegal, over and over, until the UAW found itself holding its first fair election in decades.

When the dust settled, Shawn Fain was president and he led the union to an unprecedented simultaneous strike against all of the Big Three automakers, shutting down US car production. After six weeks on the line, all three employers had capitulated, and the autoworkers had new contracts.

These contracts are noteworthy not merely for the protections they offer to workers—just as interesting is the fact that these contracts all expire in 2028.

In fact, Fain has called on all US unions bargaining for

a new contract to set a 2028 expiry date. That way, every union in the country will be able to go on strike simultaneously: a general strike. This is a clever hack around the Taft-Hartley Act's prohibition on sympathy striking, and the fact that the strike is set to arrive in the midst of the next presidential election is especially important.

Organized labor has a long history of successfully resisting fascist and crypto-fascist regimes. (There's a reason fascists attack unions as soon as they take power.) The current labor surge dates back to the first Trump administration, when teachers across the country walked off the job in a wave of #RedForEd strikes that won historical gains for teachers and their communities, with contracts that reached far beyond the economic welfare of teachers and into key justice issues for the communities they served.

For example, the Los Angeles teachers' strike won not only wage and working-conditions concessions for teachers, it also won significant gains for human rights (a ban on ICE patrols scooping up parents at the school gates) and environmental justice (money to put a green space on the grounds of, or in the immediate vicinity of, every Los Angeles school). What's more, the teachers who were unified by that strike also turned out door-knockers and organizers who delivered swing seats to the Democrats in 2018, securing a congressional majority.

Unions get stuff done, even in the midst of authoritarian chaos and crackdowns. If teachers can use labor organizing to secure gains for their students' families and communities, tech workers can use labor organizing to secure their users' interests. Disenshittification can be a union demand.

To the extent that tech workers have addressed these issues in their workplace, it has been through social movements, not labor organizing. Social movements do important work; I've devoted most of my life to them. But social movements tend to thrive under liberal regimes, even when those regimes let down their goals.

Think of how Black Lives Matter and Occupy arose under Barack Obama. His administration was hardly a friend to working people, but it didn't threaten daily survival the way the Trump administration does. People who tried to form social movements under Trump—like the Women's March—found themselves splitting their time between just trying to get through the day and trying to hold Trump's feet to the fire.

Labor organizing produces institutions, solidarity, and mutual aid—everything from strike pay to communications infrastructure. Rebuilding worker power and bringing it to the tech sector is a big project, but support for unions and worker interest in joining unions has never been higher. The future is there for unions, if we want it.

Not every union is well managed, and union leaders can undermine their members' interests in many ways. It's not just the naked corruption of the old guard at the UAW.

In 2022, the Communications Workers of America—which had made excellent inroads organizing tech workplaces—endorsed the controversial merger of Microsoft (a convicted monopolist) with the gigantic and notoriously brutal Activision Blizzard (an unconvicted monopolist). The union did so after Microsoft promised "nonaggression" toward organizers seeking to sign up the downtrodden workers of the games industry, whose workplace depredations are legendary.

This was a gross miscalculation. The Microsoft/Activision Blizzard merger significantly reduced competition in the already concentrated games industry—a giant industry that out-grosses movies, music, and TV combined.

CWA leaders assumed that Microsoft would keep its word. This was a naive assumption indeed—Microsoft is too big to fail, which means it's too big to care. Within months of the merger's completion, Microsoft had taken an axe to Blizzard's ranks, mass-firing workers, including those who were undergoing union drives.

Unions don't just represent the workers who pay their dues; they represent labor, in solidarity, against the forces of capital. To support their members effectively, unions can't confine themselves to fighting the employer—they have to fight corporate power itself.

Unionizing tech workers is a big lift, but tech labor organizers—like the people doing excellent work at Tech Solidarity and the Tech Workers Coalition—aren't on their own. There's a huge wave of unionization waiting to happen, at all kinds of workplaces, and each successful union drive and strike helps every drive and strike that comes after.

In 2024, the legendary union organizer Jane McAlevey died of cancer. McAlevey was a devastatingly effective union organizer. She was trained by organizers who came down in a direct line from the activists working in the years when unionization was criminalized and union organizers faced violent retaliation, prison, and even assassination.

McAlevey never tired of reminding workers that the legal support for unions, including the National Labor Relations Act, came after years of ultimately successful union organizing. Labor law exists because unions demanded it. Labor law didn't make unions—first we got unions, then we got labor law.

In the first week of his second term, Donald Trump effectively shuttered the NLRB, violating procedures by firing a Democratic board member named Gwynne Wilcox, leaving the NLRB without a quorum, unable to make new rules or pursue new investigations or enforcement actions. He also killed all existing NLRB enforcement actions and investigations, effectively mothballing the agency.

But Trump made a mistake. He thinks that by getting rid of the referee, he can halt the game. But all he's done is get rid of the rules. The NLRB didn't just limit what bosses could do to workers—it limited what workers could do to bosses.

The era before the NLRB was a time when bosses scurried from their mansions to their fancy restaurants to their opera boxes surrounded by armed guards. It was a time of bombings, arson, and firefights. The aphorism "War is politics by other means" (a loose translation of the military theorist Carl von Clausewitz's words) has a corollary: Politics is war by other means. The labor wars were turned into a long peace thanks to the NLRB. Now it's war. Again.

REJECT TECHNO-FIXES

POLITICAL PROBLEMS NEED POLITICAL SOLUTIONS

MIKE PEPI

IN 2006, RESIDENTS IN BERKELEY, California, started to hear about a new service that promised to revolutionize civic life. It was a new website called Kitchen Democracy. Their pitch went something like this: People are busy. Not everyone can go to a city hall meeting. Others hate speaking in public. And yet, people care about their streets, garbage, land use, and all the other decisions that make up public life.

The founders of Kitchen Democracy set out to create a digital platform whereby anyone with an internet connection could log on and participate in local politics. From 2006 to 2009, Kitchen Democracy was the "on-line forum for civic engagement" for Berkeley-area citizens. It was relatively novel for its time, even for the East Bay Area that was near the cradle of Silicon Valley. Users could register online, log in—often anonymously—and instantly see a host of local issues listed as open topics. "Can't make it to city hall tonight?" read one welcome message on its website, "Say it on Kitchen Democracy." Topic headlines included, "Rent Control Reform? Is it time to reform Berkeley's rent control laws?" There was a polling function, too.

The stated goals of Kitchen Democracy were hard to quibble with. Inconvenient city hall meetings were the problem to be solved. And the implicit goal was to use technology to increase involvement in local politics. Who wouldn't want to shine a light on the way city hall made decisions? Greater participation in decisions was generally accepted as a public good. And digital tools might get us there. Kitchen Democracy wasn't a big evil platform. It was active when Facebook was less than two years old, and still confined to college campuses. Google was yet to take control of the search market. While Kitchen Democracy wasn't a monopolistic platform, its interaction with the public sphere foreshadowed the core components of how software would come to eat the world.

But soon enough, there was a backlash. In a letter to the editor of *The Berkeley Daily Planet*, a resident accused Kitchen Democracy of misrepresenting online tallies as real votes. An issue presented through Kitchen Democracy was not an accurate reflection of the will of the people, despite in certain cases the city council treating it as such. Kitchen Democracy was a private website where you had to go voluntarily, sort of like a bulletin board. It wasn't the official organ of power, nor was it a formal decision-making body.

"As a bulletin board enterprise, it belongs to the category of petition, and not of vote," the reader wrote. Calling it a "political sleight of hand," the public comment pointed to the inherent incongruence that is created when an anonymous, voluntary account is hosted by a private, partial online community and is foisted onto the actual public sovereign institution that has its own formal process for governance.

While Kitchen Democracy sought "to bring more people into the political process through online polls" and "virtual town meetings," they did so at a civic cost. For one, it overrepresented wealthy citizens who were more likely to use personal technology. Second, it created a hierarchy that privileged those issues where users left comments, and by the simple nature that not everyone had signed up for the service, it over inflated the importance of issues that Kitchen Democracy users focused on, misrepresenting the true civic whole.

What is the legitimate role of private technology forums in civic participation? Online systems cater to a new type of user who, "openly deplore the unpleasantness of politicking," and instead create infrastructure that "treat politics as a source of personal validation and emotional succor." Kitchen Democracy was what she called a form of therapeutic politics.

Kitchen Democracy started with the noblest of intentions. Yet the experiment showed that no matter how aligned a digital platform's incentives are with the underlying institution it claims to augment, there will always be something altered. In this case, it was the role of personal agency in collective decision-making institution of city hall. Digital platforms afford a kind of sociality that privilege some forms of interaction over others. And these subtle design choices affect the institutions they aim to augment in meaningful ways. In almost all cases, the platform scaffolding that tries to improve an institution opens it up to a new register of power, a new surface area for optimization, or a new type of interpolation of its users—very few of which end up serving the individual. Kitchen Democracy displayed the original sin of the internet software—the notion that adding modes of interaction through datafication is a virtue unto itself.

Therapeutic politics like this took place on a massive scale as social media platforms like Twitter, Facebook, and Instagram allowed us to feel satisfied by virtue signaling online. Posting a black square for Black Lives Matter protests, performative hashtag activism, or arguing politics with bots designed to farm engagement on Twitter. Social media platforms enabled us to sacrifice little while providing ourselves with the feeling that we were in the right. Beyond raising awareness and inflating our sense of righteousness, the only thing we were changing was the algorithm that governed our feed. But we felt like we were making a difference. In the end, the *appearance* of democracy was the real product on offer.

Kitchen Democracy's role in fostering therapeutic politics was an early object lesson in how techno-fixes wrought unintended damage, something doomed to be repeated any time digital networks made ham-fisted incursion to usurp the role formerly served by institutions.

Almost twenty years later, the techno-fix is the order of the day: if the customer is satisfied, and the product is doing its job, then little care is paid to the cause of our problems. If anything, the public's trust was weakened. But civic virtues like public trust aren't important to the techno-fix. They are even less important to our would be cyberutopian administrators. In their version of digital utopia, it's not just that tools are the means to which we might solve problems; they are ends in themselves. Because for the utopian, anyway around the present crisis—ideally to exit the arena all together—is better than solving it on its own terms. For Kitchen Democracy, it was city hall. For more recent techno-fixes, such as blockchain and Bitcoin, the problem is the idea of the state itself. Little changed and even less was improved by the presence of Kitchen Democracy's online voting system. Say goodbye to the old world, the tool is here to save you.

Nuclear physicist Alvin Weinberg claims to have coined the term *techno-fix* in the 1960s. His primary example was his work on nuclear energy. If nuclear enginery sources could solve the energy crisis, then all the social problems related to human's competition over natural resources would wither away. Theoretically, this makes sense. But like all techno-fixes, it relies upon magical thinking: a technological breakthrough will abolish scarcity from above, and therefore abolish the need for social norms and patterns that arose to accommodate them. But when techno-fixes become applied to more acute problems, the tendency is for the issue to be treated in a limited way. Inner-city crime had been linked to warm weather, the thinking being that heat makes people more irritable and more likely to go outside. The techno-fix? Give away air conditioners in the most troubled neighborhoods. To the techno-fixer, childhood poverty was not due to the lack of available jobs or educational shortfalls, but due to families having more children than they could afford to feed. The solution: distribute IUDs to cut down on family sizes. Problem solved.

The techno-fix is a concept that is as old as technology itself. But the digital utopian takes it a step farther . Instead of treating the cause of the problem, they introduced a new digital system that ended up making the problem worse, eroding this very institution it was set out to fix. The technology critic Evgeny Morozov coined the term *solutionism* to describe the Silicon Valley belief that every problem can be solved through technological means. For Morozov, solutionism is rooted in a techno-utopian ideology that views technology as a panacea for social issues. However, this belief overlooks the complexities and nuances of problems, leading to misguided and superficial solutions that fail to address the underlying causes.

The moral calculus for the Silicon Valley platform hews toward certainty that someone has been locally satisfied in a measurable way. Innovations get immediate social credit for solving an immediate problem. They do this at the expense of the larger whole. The problem will persist, but their innovation entered the equation with certain success. Innovation gets measured at the level of the single customer, not the problem's wider reach. Consider Kitchen Democracy's killer feature: email.

With email, Kitchen Democracy users "could convey their views 'on their own schedule' without having to leave home." Private, for-profit businesses love email since it is efficient, asynchronous, and lowers the barrier to entry for transactions and communication. But the very things that make it good for business make it fundamentally unsuited for the adjudication of public affairs.

Public decision-making requires a format in which concerned citizens are gathered, equal, and properly identified as part of a collective body. The very stuff of collective decision-making relies on a participant's trust, something that is undermined by the anonymous nature of Kitchen Democracy's comments. The essence of a publicly accountable body is that its decisions are afforded debate and influence by a body of citizens sharing the same bond of responsibility and influence. Institutions of public government require this central agreement to function. Digital platforms that attempt to empower the user see the binds of this collective agreement as a nuisance, a roadblock in the way of total freedom of expression. The logic proceeds that if it is easier and faster for me to sound off on the platform, then why do we bother with the city council meetings? Providing an alternative, digital channel to express political will (via polls) serves not to extend the influence of city hall's authority but instead hollows it out by replacing the institutional authority with that of the platform. Citizens don't have to be physically present to count. Attending a public meeting via video call is okay. But executing institutional power according to the logic of the digital platform is fraught, as Kitchen Democracy's mishaps displayed. They assumed improving citizens' digital footprints would automatically augment the underlying institution. The collective nature of an open government—and by extension, democracy at large—lies in this often-minor sacrifice. The personal must ever so subtly be submitted to the greater good, even if in small symbolic gestures. The technical solution as imagined by entrepreneurs who must answer to the user, the consumer, and the digital customer misrecognizes personal satisfaction as the ultimate virtue of the virtual polis.

Kitchen Democracy is therapeutic in that it treats the symptom. We feel left out of political decisions. It does not address the outcomes: participation in city hall votes. When we spend our time being activists online it lowers participation in existing organs of government. Meanwhile it erects new hierarchies that were never there in the first place. In some cases, these new hierarchies encourage bad behavior and discourage more palatable approaches. You're a lot less likely to yell at someone in person, especially when you find out they are your neighbor. Kitchen Democracy looked at its core problem as a lack of boots on the ground participation in local government. But it somehow saw this as a technological shortcoming, not a social one.

We can contrast Kitchen Democracy's digitally networked approach with the experience of Signal Cleveland's Documenters program. Faced with shrinking local journalism outlets, Cleveland's city council's meetings and decisions are usually passed without a trace of public knowledge or accountability. According to Pew Research Center, between 2008 and 2017, newsrooms have declined by 45 percent. Cleveland's own *The Plain Dealer* (once the largest newspaper in Ohio), has been steadily shrinking through layoffs over the past decade.

To address this gap, Signal Cleveland trains and organizes people to serve as paid staff that attend important city government meetings and document their proceedings. This nonprofit newsroom isn't flashy. The focus is on simple, easy-to-read, meeting summaries. Hardly the kind of stuff that attracts clicks in the days of the attention hacking social media platform. A recent post by documenter Mary Clark reads, "$1.4 million teed up for community-based justice efforts in Cuyahoga County." It includes a downloadable PDF with bullet points from the Public Safety and Justice Affairs Committee meeting.

Notably, Signal Cleveland's solution isn't focused on using web-based technology to create an empowered user, it focuses its innovation on the institution of journalism itself, aiming for a more informed citizen. This is not to say that the online world is any less real than the physical world, or that statements made over social media don't carry the same weight as things said in person. It is to show the core problem of the techno-fix: when engineers attempt to prevent a negative outcome (in Kitchen Democracy's case, waning participation in local politics) but end up ignoring the more complex causes of the problem in the first place.

Signal Cleveland, on the other hand, uses digital technology to publish their reports—but they do not employ a technological intervention to try to circumnavigate the city hall meeting itself. Nor do they promise to the users of a new web property that their online interactions will have any impact. With Signal Cleveland, you might learn about a city hall law online, but it's meant to get you to the next meeting to have your voice heard.

The impact is real: a recent report recounts a meeting where several documenters were in attendance. Seeing this, one council member interrupted a government worker who was presenting and encouraged them to speak in a manner more comprehensible to citizens instead of using impenetrable jargon. "We have documenters here."

Signal Cleveland takes no shortcuts. There is no efficiency gained by way of some datafication, optimization, or new connections on social media. Here, "a more open and connected world" or a "cyberspace meta-town hall" is simply a better version of the institutions right in front of us. Signal Cleveland took the simple route to improving the institution—by interacting with it in a way that supports its purpose, not one that seeks to sidestep it.

"In my opinion the political problems significantly dwarf the technical problems, and the technical ones are not exactly a piece of cake either." Computer and network security researcher Marcus J. Ranum starts an infamous mailing list entry on blocking offensive material with firewalls with what he calls, "Ranum's Law of Making People Behave." Ranum's law, in a word, is a call for institutions. Specifically, bodies of governance that are not compiled of software but of laws. Software and code are a symbol for rules. Code, which shares a synonym for laws for good reason, executes commands, manipulates data, and governs its software components, granting users rights. There is much they share, but software code is limited in its ability to enact the social fabric of an institution. Here we mean a body which locates the human behavior it finds objectionable and, with human acts, punishes this behavior. This is a cultural formation, and has trouble being done by purely computational means.

The techno-fix, on the other hand, tries to escape this layer. The techno-fix that Ranum's client was hoping for would ideally automate this process by way of the scalable efficiency of network protocols. "Organizations attempt the technological route because they lack sufficient moral confidence to tackle the matter head on."

The techno-fix looks back on the shallow and narrow path to stop an outcome without ever confronting what might be causing it several steps down the chain. To the engineering mind, the simplest solution is the most elegant. But simplicity as a virtue belies the social state of problems in far too many situations for this kind of ethic of solutioning to serve as a widespread style of governance.

This is because digital technology has from the beginning sought to obviate the need for the political. The techno-fix is its greatest legacy. In a society of consumer products, the techno-fix will never tell you the cause of the problem if it cannot be solved by new consumption. Instead, it feigns control with personalized hacks at the last mile of a broader issue. Techno-utopians are unwilling to appeal to our better nature. their viewpoint is defeatist, nihilist, and cedes that some problems will always exist. Life is nasty, brutish, and short. Why solve the rot when you can monetize it?

Today's techno-determinist sees everything as an engineering problem, and not without cultural support. In the zero-interest-rate period, a key component of Silicon Valley ideology purposefully conflated the political with the technical as a side effect of their marketing claims. Drunk on the market's fictitious need for constant solutions, and with a vague zeitgeist enthralled on consumer devices and social platforms, so-called revolutionary ideas foisted on the political imagination were not ideas as much as they were products. Once the digitization of everyday life was nearly complete, negative externalities reared their ugly head. Instead of going back to reconsider the root assumption that Silicon Valley could solve any of these political problems, we double down on technical fixes to patch the failures of the previous techno-fix. In the face of diminished socialization for seniors, we were handed virtual reality headsets. Increased male loneliness due to too much screen time: How about AI girlfriends? Would it not make more sense to investigate why there is a crisis in senior living or to better understand why men have increasingly reported difficulty finding companions? Why do we only solve the ills of the platform by way of tweaking the organizing machines, by way of new technical innovation, or by way of inventing a new more technologically complex economic flow? Our first reaction was to crown a new technological patch where an account of the political missteps might better serve us.

Under this affliction, solutions to problems react to the most immediate negative form or the proximate state of degradation; the trade-off is that the political will that forms around such solutions loses all sense of the first-order roots of the problem. I call this *proximate cause political amnesia*. When solutions myopically focus on the most proximate cause, they tend to solve a problem that was only recently (and newly) created by the last failed solution. The result is that the causes of the root problem are erased from the problem set altogether.

Proximate cause political amnesia is why techno-fixes are proposed at first blush. The ensuing debate is so preoccupied in implementation discussions on the merits of this innovation or that techno-fix that we not only table any political remedy in the first place but we entirely discount that the problem is itself one created by nontechnical, political machinations that themselves predate the tools at our disposal. Political problems need political solutions.

TAX THE RICH

RAY D. MADOFF

THE UNITED STATES HAS ALLOWED MANY of its wealthiest individuals to quietly secede from the country that benefits them financially. As the richest one percent of Americans have come to control more than thirty percent of the country's wealth, the tax code has given them the tools to abdicate their responsibilities and, in a sense, to relocate to a tax-free version of American life—a wealth island of sorts.

While millions of working Americans pay substantial portions of their resources to support the expenses of the country—its social safety net, national defense, interest on the national debt, and the myriad other expenses needed to support the most economically developed country in the world—the individuals on wealth island are insulated from such workaday burdens by a tax system that imposes little or no tax on their most common sources of wealth: investments and inheritances. Their ability to avoid taxes in those areas allows their wealth and power to grow unabated and exponentially.

For over one hundred years, this country has operated under a system explicitly designed to impose its greatest burdens on those with the greatest capacity to pay. It is natural for people to believe that the combination of the income tax imposed at progressive rates and the additional estate tax imposed on the richest Americans accomplishes that result. While some may cheat, it is not the system that looks to be at fault.

The tax lives of the rich in the twenty-first century are very different from what the rules appear to provide.

While the progressive income tax and the estate tax remain on the books, they no longer accomplish what they were designed to do or what they once did. For those with wealth, taxes are someone else's problem.

While taxes on the richest Americans have become largely elective, the country has accrued a crushing national debt that threatens its ability to meet its most basic expenses. Even more troubling than the fiscal implications is the fact that the country has become a land of two people rather than one: overburdened workers at all income levels carrying the lion's share of the costs of running the country and a growing American aristocracy of wealth and power who are allowed to abdicate their responsibilities to the nation.

For wealthy Americans, maintaining the current system means maintaining a tax code rife with permissive loopholes. Addressing the problem must likewise be centered on the tax code. The natural answer would be to reinvigorate the estate tax, the one tax specifically aimed at the richest Americans.

However, judging by the recent past, this seems

exceedingly unlikely to occur: Congress has not closed a single loophole in the estate tax since 1990, even as the tax has become ever more hollowed out by a growing panoply of tax-avoidance techniques.

One reason for this failure to act is the effectiveness of the public relations campaign, which began in the 1990s, to destroy the legitimacy of the estate tax. This campaign effectively transformed public perception of the tax, from an innocuous backstop to the income tax that added progressivity to the tax system, into an immoral double tax imposed on people at their moment of greatest vulnerability—death.

But history shows that there are other factors, not just effective public relations, that make it unlikely imposing extra taxes specifically geared to the richest Americans (including the estate tax, or more recent proposals for a wealth tax) will be adopted today.

The most consequential tax reforms in the history of the US have occurred when the country's economic system was under threat—specifically, the threat of socialism and communism and their appeals to the working class. For much of the twentieth century, these threats played a critical role in the adoption and expansion of special taxes applied to the very wealthy, imposed as a way of promoting legitimacy for the capitalist order.

With the disappearance of socialism and communism from the twenty-first-century political landscape, such threats against capitalism have largely disappeared. Another factor that has tempered the possibility of an updated tax system is the changing nature of war, especially the shift from mass conscription to an all-volunteer professional military.

The original estate tax was adopted and expanded amid US involvement in World Wars I and II, during decades when the American working class sacrificed life and livelihood to secure the political fate of the country.

The adoption and expansion of an estate tax was one way the country showed its public some measure of reciprocity. Countries have been most likely to impose taxes on the rich at times of war as a way for the rich to be subject to conscriptions of wealth, while the rest of the country was subject to conscriptions of men. As countries like the US have moved away from mass conscriptions toward a volunteer army, they are far less likely to feel the need to impose taxes specifically geared to the rich.

The face of wealth in the twenty-first century is different, and differently perceived, than it used to be. At the height of the Gilded Age, the superrich lived in a way that was wholly alien to the average American worker, who peered into opulent New York ballrooms in the same way that we may gaze into a zoo enclosure today. Progressive leaders accused these robber barons and their families of attempting to make a new class of American aristocrats, warning that their newly forming band of economic royalty was dangerous for the nation.

The superrich fed the public's accusations of royal aspirations with their homes and ballrooms modeled after foreign palaces; their exhibition of grandiose tiaras and diamond-encrusted dresses; and their armies of servants dressed in the livery of European aristocracy.

Unlike their Gilded Age forebears, the modern superrich have increasingly shied away from exhibiting their riches as a measure of status. In fact, they now appear to conspicuously avoid it. As the top hats and tiaras of a century ago have been replaced with tennis shoes and quarter-zips, the visible trappings of wealth have merged with those of the middle class; the wealthy and the not wealthy today dress like each other.

Warren Buffett, with his lunches at McDonald's and famously frayed ties (prompting Obama to give him a new one to wear during his White House visit), embodies an older version of this look. Elon Musk has publicly embraced a more youthful "everyman" style of T-shirts under blazers, an affectation he famously burnished while smoking cannabis live on the *The Joe Rogan Experience* podcast.

Of course, many wealthy continue to engage in behavior that meets the old definitions of conspicuous consumption, flying private jets to kids' soccer practices and living in mansions that would put even the Vanderbilt estate to shame. However, unlike the palaces on Fifth Avenue, these mega-mansions are increasingly sequestered from the rest of America, in neighborhoods and entire communities segregated by economics. The days of peering through the glass walls of palatial estates to watch diamond-studded debutantes are gone, replaced by the gatehouses of private communities and the brandless athleisure uniforms that disguise their inhabitants.

Things have changed for the middle class as well. The post–World War II era was a time of rising wages and a highly egalitarian wage structure (sometimes referred to as the Great Compression), buttressed by expansive social programs, new lending programs, and the development of cheap housing for returning American GIs. This created a situation in which regular working Americans could afford to enjoy a version of the lifestyle that had once been the sole purview of the rich: home ownership, college educations, automobiles, and vacations.

Since the end of the twentieth century, middle-class Americans have been finding it increasingly difficult to obtain what were once viewed as middle-class staples with their earnings alone. Home ownership, in particular, has become a fundamentally important form of wealth creation for middle-class families, meaning that rising housing prices, especially in urban centers, has hamstrung an entire new generation of prospective middle-class Americans who are unable to buy a home.

With the margins tightening, research shows many Americans now believe inheritance is one of the only viable ways to achieve the quality of life enjoyed by their forebears.

As inheritance has become seen as a prerequisite to living the middle-class dream, many middle-class Americans have bought into the idea that limits on inheritances are a threat to their economic security. This is a grand victory for the public relations apparatus that recast the estate tax as a predatory "death tax" affecting everyone, but it also represents a fundamental misunderstanding of the current nature of the estate tax. A poll conducted in 2017 found that sixty-three percent of respondents believed the estate tax predominantly affected poor and middle-class families—a belief far from the reality, as more than ninety-nine percent of such estates are untaxed by the federal government.

All this suggests that special taxes specifically geared to the wealthy—like estate taxes or wealth taxes—are less likely to be embraced by the American public than one might expect. But there is another way forward to bring the country together to share the costs of our democracy, and that is to reform the broad-based income tax to bring in the most common sources of wealth for America's ultra-wealthy: their investments and inheritances.

A precursor to doing so would be to introduce honesty into the debate about who carries the costs of government. Across countries and throughout history, the wealthiest people have always sought to avoid taxes to preserve their wealth and power. The French aristocracy did so directly, through explicit rules that excluded them from the reach of taxes. However, this type of explicit exclusion is unlikely to work in a democracy based on principles of equality where preferential tax avenues for the rich must be hidden from public view.

By concealing their highly lucrative paths to tax avoidance, wealthy people have succeeded in maintaining secrecy about their actual tax liabilities. If one wished to find out how much tax those with high wealth (as opposed to those with high income) pay—or don't pay—the information would be surprisingly difficult to find.

One reason is because the most accurate source of information about how much people pay—actual tax returns—are protected from public scrutiny by strict privacy laws. This stands in sharp contrast to a brief period in the early part of the twentieth century, when the richest individuals and corporations had their names and tax liabilities published on the front page of the *New York Times*.

This modern secrecy was at least partially lifted in 2022, when the IRS employee Charles Littlejohn leaked data to journalists, giving them access to a vast cache of tax returns of the richest Americans. The series of ProPublica stories that followed revealed how many of America's wealthiest citizens—including Michael Bloomberg, Jeff Bezos, George Soros, and Elon Musk—paid little or nothing in taxes.

While these stories should have been enough to shift people's understanding about who does and does not pay taxes, the response to the leak was muted by a barrage of articles about the propriety of ProPublica's actions in publishing the tax information and by statistics around income taxes paid by those with high incomes. These responses, which inaccurately conflated the tax burdens of those with high incomes and those with great wealth, sought to portray the ProPublica stories as deviations from some larger norm in which the rich were doing their part.

Consider the case of a person with a $1 million salary (subject to roughly $370,000 in income taxes) who also receives a $100 million inheritance. Under current reporting rules, only the $1 million salary is reported, giving the impression—to the taxpayer, the IRS, and the public at large—that the taxpayer with $1 million in income will pay taxes at a rate of thirty-seven percent. Were the taxpayer required to report the $100 million inheritance as well, it would be easy to see that the actual total tax burden would be less than one percent of the income acquired in that year.

These reporting systems are also puzzlingly scattershot. Whereas the receipt of the inheritance in our example does not require reporting, other types of income—even income not subject to tax—does require reporting. Income from tax-exempt bonds, distributions from Roth IRAs, and capital gains on the sale of a house must all be reported on taxpayers' annual tax returns, even though they are not subject to tax.

The lack of good public information about how much tax the wealthy pay has facilitated the proliferation of false and misleading statistics. The most powerful and often-cited statistic states that the top one percent of income earners pay almost forty percent of all income taxes, while the bottom forty percent of earners pay no income taxes at all. Such statistical accounts are often used in misleading ways by conflating high earners with high wealth owners.

While it is true that these high-income earners do indeed pay the most income taxes, it says nothing about the wealthiest Americans, who—because of their ability to avoid taxable income, particularly for their investments and inheritances—are just as likely to be in the bottom forty percent of income earners who pay no taxes as they are in the top one percent.

A final source of misinformation has been public communication about the nature of payroll taxes. The failure to describe payroll taxes as real taxes may have been valuable in terms of securing the political viability of the Social Security system in its early days, and no doubt makes it more resistant to political change, but it has also served to distort the public's perception about who pays the costs of running the country's most expensive programs, its social insurance programs.

We are no longer living in the days of Coxey's Army when the vulnerabilities of old-age disability and unemployment were seen as something we should all manage for ourselves. Instead, the protections provided by Social Security and Medicare are essential features of a modern economy, and workers should be recognized for the costs they carry in providing them.

An intellectually honest discussion of what the tax system does for wealthy people would be a victory in itself. Making progress beyond that would require a set of solutions to reverse the damage that has been done and to recalibrate the US tax system as something other than an apparatus for consolidating wealth. However, this goal is not beyond reach.

The path to doing so involves three steps: (1) repealing the estate tax, (2) bringing inheritances and investments into the income tax system, and (3) reforming the rules around philanthropy to strengthen the charitable sector, while ensuring that everyone plays a role in supporting the country's expenses.

The revenue the estate tax now raises (only $30 billion in 2024, less than 0.5 percent of the country's total revenue) is minuscule, an amount so small that Elon Musk could gain or lose it over the course of a day and not notice the difference. And the continuing power of large inheritances to persist through generations is seen in the annual Forbes 400 list, on which a full thirty percent of those listed appear simply due to luck of birth.

Meanwhile, as the estate tax accomplishes none of its goals, its continued existence produces affirmative harms, principal among which is its sowing of a distorted public understanding about the actual tax burden borne by the wealthiest Americans. Unlike payroll taxes, which are largely hidden from public view but disproportionally burden those at the other end of the wealth distribution, the estate tax has been front and center for an American public that has been made hyperaware of it from the anti-tax campaign that began in the late 1990s and continues today. The effect of this hyperawareness of the estate tax is to provide a protective shield for the rich, making the public believe that rich Americans pay not just one set of taxes, but two.

The income tax has conspicuously avoided the most common sources of wealth of the richest Americans:

inheritances and investments. In other words, the existence of the estate tax has served to legitimate the shortcomings of the income tax system.

When a lucky heir receives a windfall inheritance or gift, that is just as much income as are earnings, lottery winnings, prize money, or money found on the street—all of which are subject to income taxes at the highest ordinary rates. A system that requires someone who earns $100,000 to pay almost thirty percent in payroll and income taxes while giving another person who inherits $10 million a free pass is indefensible—which is why the system relies so heavily on misinformation.

Although the tax code does not explicitly exclude investment gains from the income tax, the results are the same as if it did. Through techniques like buy, borrow, die—which allows owners of wealth to defer taxes on gains until they are sold and, accordingly, to avoid taxes altogether by holding investments until death—the evasion of income taxes is institutionalized.

The income tax plays an important role in American life. Of all the taxes, it regularly provides the most revenue to the country, and in 2024, the amount that it raised—$2.43 trillion—constituted almost half of all government revenue. Because of the requirement to file annual tax returns, income tax is the tax with which Americans are most familiar. And tellingly, because of the country's heavy dependence on the income tax system, it is one of the few taxes that gets regular attention from Congress.

Two simple reforms can solve this problem: Tax the receipt of inheritances and gifts under the income tax system (allowing for certain transfers to occur tax-free), and tax unrealized gains at death on the final income tax return of the decedent.

Repeal the exclusion for inheritances and gifts: Objectively, money received as gifts and inheritances fits within the parameters of the income tax, which applies broadly (to quote the tax code) to "all income from whatever source derived." The reason it is not subject to tax, however, is that a different section of the code says that "gross income does not include the value of property acquired by gift, bequest, devise, or inheritance."

By repealing this exclusion (in conjunction with

repealing the estate tax), the entire tax code would be fairer while also bringing the wealthy into the purview of the same tax system that applies to the vast majority of Americans.

There are several reasons taxing inheritances as income would be preferable to taxing inheritances through the estate tax system:

First, taxing inheritances as income fits in with people's basic understanding of the income tax. The exclusion of gifts and inheritances is an anomaly to this comprehensive system and one that many people don't even know exists. Many people mistakenly assume that large gifts and inheritances are already subject to income tax.

Second, taxing inheritances to heirs rather than estates gets away from the perception that the estate tax is an unfair double tax imposed on dead people. Both estate taxes and inheritance taxes are borne financially by the recipient of the property, who receives that property only after taxes have been paid. Taxes imposed on heirs upon the receipt of property are far less vulnerable to such charges.

To accommodate parents' common desire to provide basic support for their children, and to allow for people to support each other without government interference, the income tax on gifts and inheritances could provide the same exclusions currently available for gift tax purposes; these allow for property to pass tax-free to spouses and also for people to provide educational and medical expenses, as well as $18,000 per year to anyone else, tax-free. In addition, the rule could allow each person to inherit up to $1 million and pay income taxes only on anything in excess of that.

As for family businesses, the rules could provide an exception for family farms and businesses of moderate size (perhaps subject to a $20 million cap) for those heirs actively involved in the business. But any such exception must be mindful that what works well for moderate estates would be harmful if allowed for large ones.

There is no reason we should promote the creation of dynastic wealth by giving a free pass on taxes as multi-billion-dollar businesses—like Walmart, Koch Industries, and Mars—get passed from generation to generation, particularly because of the way that wealth passed this way magnifies political power.

As the tax scholar James Repetti has written:

> It is one thing to deal with a more powerful person than yourself; it is another to consider that your children will have to deal with the children of the powerful person, and that your grandchildren will have to deal with her grandchildren.
>
> In its worst form, of course, this creates a royalty, a concern addressed in a famous quote attributed to Alexis de Tocqueville: "What is most important for democracy is not that great fortunes should not exist, but that great fortunes should not remain in the same hands."

Our experience with families with dynastic wealth undermining the estate tax provides good evidence of the problems dynastic wealth can create.

There are many practical reasons for not taxing unrealized gains during life, most notably due to the difficulty of valuation and also problems raised by potential lack of liquidity, if people have to pay tax on unrealized gains.

However, while these justifications make a lot of sense during a person's life, they no longer do once that person has given up ownership.

Both President Nixon and President Obama proposed that, to create a fairer tax system that treats investment income more like income from earnings, gains should be taxed upon the transfer of property by gift or at death. This rule was adopted in Canada, and we should do so here to ensure that those gains are taxed to the person who earned them.

Just looking at the Forbes 400 list, there are hundreds of billions, and perhaps even trillions, of dollars in untaxed gains. Recent research from the Brookings Institution suggests that as much as one-third of all bequeathable wealth comprises unrealized gains. There is no reason for the American tax system to give owners of those profits a free pass.

Tax rules governing philanthropy are also in need of reform. Charities play an essential role in American society, and we need to make sure that they have the resources they need to do their work. At the same time, the government needs to have the resources it needs to do its work. The rules of philanthropy should be reformed to accomplish both goals.

This is not the first time this work has been done. The 1969 rules—treating public charities differently from private foundations—put a comprehensive system in place designed to ensure that charitable dollars made their way to charitable ends within a reasonable period. But the rise of donor-advised funds has made it easy to evade those rules.

To address this, Congress should impose meaningful payout rules on donor-advised fund accounts (not on sponsors who can easily game the rules) and private foundations to make clear that contributions to donor-controlled intermediaries are not the same as outright donations to working charities.

Finally, Congress should impose limits on charitable tax benefits for capital gains and estate and gift tax purposes that are similar to those imposed in the income tax world. For example, if Warren Buffett transfers $100 billion to his kids' private foundation, the charitable deduction could be limited to fifty percent, ensuring that at least some of his wealth is subject to tax so it can be used to meet some of the expenses of government. In this way, wealthy donors will still be able to commit their funds for the public good while a portion of their money goes to sharing the costs of government.

Unlike prerevolutionary France, the US was founded on principles of equality. These principles, though incomplete at conception, have served as a continuing guide for the ongoing process of building a more perfect union. Bringing the rich back into the tax system is an essential step in this ongoing endeavor.

RESIST BILLIONAIRES

CHUCK COLLINS

AN ECONOMY RIGGED TO FUNNEL SO MUCH wealth and power to the billionaire class is bad for you and everyone else. It undermines your life in some major ways. Here are ten ways you are personally getting burned by billionaires:

(1) *The billionaires stick you with their tax bill.* By opting out of their tax obligations, the billionaire class shifts responsibility on to you to pay for everything from

infrastructure to national defense to veterans' services.

(2) *They rob you of your voice and vote.* With the billionaire capture of the government, what you think barely matters. Your vote might still make a difference, but only in marginal situations where the billionaires haven't dominated candidate selection, campaign finance, and policy priorities. The billionaires love gridlock and government shutdowns because they can block popular legislation from happening.

(3) *The billionaires supercharge the housing crisis—and profit from it.* Billionaire demand for luxury housing is driving up the cost of land and housing construction, supercharging the already existing housing crisis. Billionaire speculators are buying up rental housing, single-family homes, and mobile-home parks to squeeze more money out of the housing shortage. Global billionaires are coming to "tax haven USA" to park their money in U.S. farmland, timber, and housing.

(4) *They inflame existing divisions in society.* The billionaires don't want you to understand how they are picking your pocket. So, they invest heavily—pouring millions into partisan media organizations and divisive

politicians—to deflect our attention away from their harmful behavior. Their divisive policy and social agenda drives down wages, worsens the historic racial wealth divide, and scapegoats immigrants.

(5) *They trash your environment*. The billionaires are the super polluters and carbon emitters, burning up the earth with their excessive consumption through yachts, private jets, and multiple mansions. While you're recycling and walking, they are zooming around in private jets and yachts with the carbon emissions and pollution of small nation-states. While we all need to do our part, billionaires make us feel like chumps for making ecological choices and sacrifices.

(6) *They make you sick*. Billionaire-backed private-equity funds are buying up hospitals and health specialties—along with big pharma drug companies—with the aim of squeezing more out of health care consumers. Health outcomes in societies with extreme disparities in wealth are worse for everyone, even the rich, than societies with less inequality.

(7) *They block timely action on climate change*. Fossil-fuel billionaires spend millions to block the transition to

a healthy future. They fund politicians to declare a bogus energy emergency to keep their coal plants open and shut down competing wind projects. They are running out the clock for our governments to take action to avert the worst impacts of climate disruption.

(8) *They are coming for your pets.* Billionaire private equity funds know we love our pets like family members and are sometimes willing to go into debt for their health care. To squeeze more money out of us, the billionaires are buying up veterinary care, medical specialties, pet food and supply—and even pet care services like Rover.com.

(9) *They dictate what's on your dinner plate.* The food barons—billionaires that monopolize almost every sector of the food economy—are dictating the price, ingredients, and supply of most foodstuffs.

(10) *They are corrupting charity and philanthropy.* Billionaire philanthropy has become a taxpayer-subsidized form of private power and influence. As philanthropy gets more top-heavy—with most charity dollars flowing from the ultra-wealthy—it distorts and warps the independence of the nonprofit sector.

(11) Bonus: *They are buying up and hijacking the media.* The billionaires are buying up the media: broadcast, social media, news outlets. We need more news and social media outlets that are independent of billionaires.

There's a lot we can do together to fight the billionaire hijacking of our society and democracy. Talk to your neighbors about the ways they are feeling the billionaire burn. Don't act alone. Join with others.

RESIST NATIONALISM

REJECT PROTECTIONISM

HARSHA WALIA

CALLS FOR NATIONALIST PROTECTIONISM against neoliberal globalization have only emboldened the far right and heightened anti-migrant xenophobia. Far-right organizations are even weaponizing resistance to fascism as a nationalist cause.

In France, anti-immigration and Islamophobic forces present themselves as a new resistance, a direct reference to forces that fought Nazi occupation. Similarly, Italian resistance to Nazi occupation is being memorialized and shaped by far-right forces in that country as a white patriotic movement—nationalist at its core—fighting foreign occupation. This conveniently erases the more than fifty nationalities, including thousands of migrants in Italy, represented in the internationalist resistance against the Nazis and Mussolini's fascism. The anticolonial dimension of the resistance is also omitted, as are those who fought Italian fascism in the colonies.

In the US, white nationalists deploy the trope of the "vanishing Indian" and appropriate Indigenous struggles to position themselves as victims of and defenders against an imagined migrant invasion. That white supremacists spuriously claim an affinity with Indigenous nations is a disgusting conflation of the nation-state with indigeneity, particularly abhorrent in contexts where Indigenous people are resisting the weight of centuries of genocidal settler colonialism. Racist nationalism in the US and other colonial states is built upon Indigenous nations and tethered to coercive power, not relationships to place or land.

Trump's fascination with Andrew Jackson illustrates how settler colonialism is the most violent form of far-right nationalism and stands in sharp contrast to Indigenous articulations of place, nationhood, kinship, and economies of reciprocity. Leanne Betasamosake Simpson imagines Indigenous futures as ones that "reject dispossession and settler colonialism and the violence of capitalism, heteropatriarchy, white supremacy, and anti-Blackness that maintains them." To her, "Indigenous nationhood is a radical and complete overturning of the nation-state's political formations."

In assessing anticolonial movements, Adom Getachew asserts that African, African American, and Caribbean nationalists were not primarily concerned with the building of nation-states. "Against the standard view of decolonization as a moment of nation-building," Getachew writes that Black anticolonial nationalism of this period was actually a global anticolonial "world-making" rooted in the principles of internationalism, nondomination, and redistribution. Simpson and Getachew point to a vision of the future beyond state formations, which uphold social control.

Anti-migrant xenophobia, immigration enforcement, detention centers, migration controls, and border securitization are ultimately the tentacles of a much-larger ideological monster: the rule of racist, nationalist borders. I align with a leftist politics of no borders, since the borders of today are completely bound up in the violences of dispossession, accumulation, exploitation, and their imbrications with race, caste, gender, sexuality, and ability. A no-borders politics is not abstract; it is grounded in the material and lived impacts of our world, scarred by warfare and warming.

Like the regime of private property, borders are not simply lines marking territory; they are the product of, and produce, social relations from which we must emancipate ourselves. The borders of advanced capitalist and imperialist states, including Australia, Canada, the EU, Israel, Japan, New Zealand, and the US, demarcate a fortress hoarding 73 percent of global wealth and only 14 percent of the world's population, and passports from these regions guarantee the most mobility worldwide.

A no-borders politics is more expansive than an open borders one; it calls on us to transform the underlying social, political, and economic conditions giving rise to what we know as "the migration crisis." A meaningful no borders politics requires an end to forced displacement caused by the brutalities of conquest, the voraciousness of capital, and the wreckages of climate change. We must wage resistance to displacement and immobility in all its forms: drone warfare, military occupations, policing agencies, mass incarceration, reservations, ghettos, gentrification, capitalist trade agreements, special economic zones, sweatshops, land grabs, resource extraction, and temporary labor programs.

Dismantling borders requires that we abandon capitalism, which has only given us the merciless expropriation of land and exploitation of labor. We need to urgently jettison regimes of private property, reject dispossessive forces of colonialism, forsake extractive labor markets, and abolish carceral regimes. To fully undo the rule of borders, we must also undo the apartheid racial-social organization subtending the criminalization of migration and upholding ethnonationalism as citizenship. A no borders politics, then, is a politics of refusal, a politics of revolution, and a politics of repair.

Revolutions stretch our imaginations and manifest our desires. Political struggle is a purpose and a practice.

In between utopic romanticism and demobilizing fatalism—both of which foreclose the future as a process we generate—is our collective commitment to revolutionary struggles blossoming around us and ushering in a different world.

Our profound planetary crisis has propelled groundswells of resistance to racial-capitalist, border imperialist, and far-right nationalist rule. Following a surge of xenophobic violence in South Africa in 2019, hundreds of refugees and migrants, mainly from the Democratic Republic of the Congo, Ethiopia, Somalia, and Zimbabwe, occupied the streets and buildings of Cape Town for six months. Many migrant domestic workers, most from Indonesia and the Philippines, joined the 2019 democracy movement in Hong Kong and organized migrant union affiliates within the Hong Kong Confederation of Trade Unions.

In the US in 2019, thousands of "Close the Camps" mobilizations, demanding closure of detention facilities incarcerating migrant children and families, swept across the country. On May Day of the following year, mostly immigrant and racialized retail, warehouse, and food service workers at Amazon, Target, Whole Foods, and Instacart led protests and strikes for higher pay and better safety protections during the Covid-19 pandemic, while also refusing a return to pre-pandemic "normalcy."

Around the same time, tens of thousands of jobless and desperate mostly caste-oppressed migrant workers and day laborers in India's major cities defied a national lockdown, thousands of them battling with police as they attempted to make their way home to their villages.

In Bosnia in early 2020, seven hundred refugees broke through the fence surrounding the Miral camp and proceeded to blockade the road leading to the Croatian border. In February 2020, on the Greek hotspot of Lesbos, over two thousand refugees revolted against their confinement on the island and the horrific conditions of malnutrition, lack of sanitation, and exposure to the cold in the camp. Though they faced riot police who fired tear gas, they chanted "Freedom! Freedom!" and marched on foot toward the capital of Lesbos.

In a brilliant stroke of metaphor, the undocumented migrants' organization Black Vests (Gilets Noirs) in France and the refugee group Black Sardines in Italy are loudly asserting their presence within the working-class

Yellow Vests and anti-Salvini Sardines social movements. Through visible protests, defiant occupations, and viral manifestos, the Black Vests and Black Sardines are revealing the real underbelly of austerity, racial capitalism, and far-right populism in Europe, just as incendiary Black-led rebellion is pushing forward abolitionist struggle in the US.

While power is omnipresent, shaping every aspect of our lives, these and other movements remind us that injustice is not ordained to determine our future. Empires crumble, capitalism is not inevitable, gender is not biology, whiteness is not immutable, prisons are not inescapable, and borders are not natural law. We can abolish the organization of difference, through citizenship, race, caste, gender, sexuality, ability, and neoliberal atomization, which underwrites relentless state and social violence despite hollow proclamations of tolerance.

We can narrow the schisms between the international working class and reimagine the working class as the capacious global proletariat, and labor—beyond the confines of accumulation and extraction—as feminist economies of care and Indigenous land stewardship. We can weave solidarities through the lens of abundance, rather than scarcity, and celebrate the interdependence of the particularities of our humanities.

We can reconstruct egalitarian social ecosystems, where we cultivate depropertied, decommodified, decarceral, decolonial, and democratic relations. Considering that millions of people are differentiated and managed under border imperialism, we can and must embrace a basic yet expansive vision: no human being is illegal.

Even as bordering practices fragment internationalist solidarities and exert seemingly totalizing power over who migrates and under which conditions, the mere existence of autonomous "illegal" migration—an expression of revolt, redistribution, and reparation—defies attempts to control it. This is our starkest reminder that man-made borders shall never fully thwart human movements compelled by the upheavals of our era.

Consider the prophetic words of Toni Morrison: "In this new space one can imagine safety without walls, can iterate difference that is prized but unprivileged, and can conceive of a third, if you will pardon the expression, world 'already made for me, both snug and wide open, with a doorway never needing to be closed.' Home." The freedom to stay and the freedom to move are revolutionary corollaries refusing imperial bordered sovereignties, with home as our shared horizon.

CONTROL YOUR FOOD

MAHA VS. MAMDANI

BY RAJ PATEL

MORE THAN A CENTURY BEFORE MAYOR Zohran Mamdani declared he wanted a New York City network of grocery stores "focused on keeping prices low," socialists in Spain were furious about a network of grocery stores that kept prices low. An archipelago of *tienda-asilos* (shelter or asylum shops) had opened across the country in 1886, offering low-cost food for the burgeoning population of urban poor people. For the store's proponents, *tienda-asilos* offered a way for working people to buy a square meal without the indignities of charity.

The Spanish Socialist Workers' Party begged to differ. First, they argued, the *tienda-asilos* were more *tienda* than *asilo*. Even though the stores themselves were nonprofit enterprises, the merchants along the supply chain providing food to the kitchen were in it for the money, and there were rumors of collusion and profiteering. (Then as now, food philanthropy was a lucrative business.) Second, there was little dignity to be had. The stores were sometimes tucked away far from town, where none need be seen queuing for a discount and the bourgeoisie needn't be troubled by the sight of urban poverty. Reports of rancid food within the stores were rife.

The Spanish socialists didn't want philanthropy and food banks; they wanted a way to eat that built class solidarity with dignity. But good examples were rare. At the turn of the century, the problem of urban hunger vexed socialist and anarchist organizers across Europe and North America. Back then, spikes in food prices were often followed by the only response available: rebellion. In 1898 in Milan, dozens were killed in bread riots brought on by high wheat prices. After poor weather and an outbreak of hoof-and-mouth disease, European food prices spiked again in 1911. Women led protests in Austria and France. This time, some municipalities were ready to help, supporting negotiations for lower prices.

While the working class was in revolt, the middle class was revolted by something entirely different in the food system: impurity. In the US, a wave of food adulteration and contamination scandals—paired with Upton Sinclair's revelations of filth in slaughterhouses and workforce exploitation in his 1905 novel, *The Jungle*—led to the passage of the Pure Food and Drugs Act of 1906. Sinclair was frustrated by the differing views over whether food should be governed as an object of charity, a commodity, or a public good.

Today, those same questions have resurfaced, energizing movements at opposite sides of the political spectrum. On one end is Mamdani's revival of the idea of a municipal grocery store, part of a long lineage of socialist efforts to build dignity. At the other is Secretary of Health and Human Services Robert F. Kennedy Jr.'s MAHA coalition. Like its counterparts on the left, MAHA too distrusts the food system, condemning additives, pesticides, and profiteering. But the links it draws between food and racial hygiene and its invocation of a natural purity that will strengthen the nation has its roots in a different source: 1930s Germany. Where it casts dignity as an individual project of vigilance, self-care, and protection from foreign bodies, Mamdani connects it with a longer tradition of collective provision.

Indeed, his public grocery proposal has a predecessor over a century old. George R. Lunn was a Presbyterian minister and member of the Socialist Party of America. In his mayoral campaign, he sought to meet Schenectady, NY's crisis of social reproduction—in which family incomes were devoured by rent, and an increasingly foreign-born workforce was at the mercy of unscrupulous bosses and traders—by providing affordable food. While campaigning, Lunn was careful to present himself as a reasonable man, a pastor and a veteran, convincingly enough to win him the election.

Once in office, Lunn was never able to surmount, as he put it, the "bitter opposition of the old parties," both Republican and Democratic. Shortly after his first term as mayor began in 1912, he opened a public grocery store in the basement of City Hall and launched a municipal attempt to sell ice at cost. Neither plan lasted. Middle-class voters abandoned him, and local retailers sued.

Although Lunn himself was never able to resuscitate it, the idea of a public grocery store refused to die. World War I inaugurated National Kitchens in the UK; in the US, the federal government mobilized state resources to manage food supplies countrywide. Together the projects signaled, for the first time, that not only municipal but state-level socialist policy might be possible for the dinner table.

During World War I, New York City entertained ideas of a municipal food department, which would use public health prerogatives to divert food from waste streams and into city-governed municipal markets. Until the private sector eroded them in the 1940s, these had been far more comprehensive, with the majority of grocery shopping conducted in public markets with regulated food safety and commercial good conduct.

Those plans never came to fruition, but the demand persisted among anarchists and socialists. In 1917 the Mothers' Anti-High Price League, a group of working-class and largely immigrant women, led mass demonstrations in New York, demanding $1 million for city-run grocery stores and another $1 million for school lunches.

The idea that the government should function not just as a regulator but as a purchaser and distributor in the food system was echoed in wartime food protests in Boston, Philadelphia, and Chicago. They took place outside the US too, especially in countries that had suffered price hikes. In Germany, revolutionary councils temporarily took over food distribution in several cities from 1918–19. In Chile, La Asamblea Obrera de Alimentación Nacional, a cross-class social movement formed in November 1918 just days after the Armistice in Europe, led twenty thousand people on a march for public food systems in Santiago.

Fifty-two years later, La Asamblea got what it wanted. Salvador Allende, a former public health minister, eked out a victory in the 1970 presidential election, winning thirty-six percent of the national vote. His party implemented a national network of Juntas de Abastecimiento y Control de Precios (Supply and Price Control Boards), and "people's stores" sprouted up across the country. Allende's Popular Unity coalition nationalized the import supply chain into one consolidated state-run firm, the Chilean National Distribution Company, as a way of building solidarity with bakers, butchers, dry goods sellers, and other small-scale food providers. Without the middleman, the company could buy at lower prices.

Allende's exercise in solidarity development didn't go far enough down the supply chain. Farmers, upset that price controls put limits on their incomes, refused to bring their wheat to market. The media was immediately hostile, too. Lacking allies in rural areas, Allende's vision foundered. Economic sabotage and a bosses' strike led to a counter-hegemonic coalition of truck drivers, upper-middle-class consumers, and large-scale traders, all of whom protested against Allende. Their efforts provided the backbone for the 1973 coup d'etat led by Augusto Pinochet who, after seizing power, dismantled the public grocery in September of that year.

I recently re-read Joshua Frens-String's stirring account of Chile's experiment, *Hungry for Revolution* (2021), because Mamdani's proposal for municipal grocery stores seemed to stir such deep emotions. Frens-String is hopeful. "Mamdani's plan has the potential to guarantee access to essential foodstuffs at a time when consumers are still experiencing rapidly rising grocery prices," he told me over email. At a large enough scale, he thought, the plan could successfully curb food price inflation "by offering a competitive check on private establishments."

The scale's the rub. At present, New York City has only six small markets, vestiges of La Guardia New Deal–era attempts to return to public markets, where the city leases stalls, and small retailers sell their wares. But large-scale models do exist. Bulgaria's government has announced plans to create a network of 1,500 stores across the country—particularly in underserved areas—with the goal of providing affordable groceries (with a maximum ten percent mark-up) and supporting small-scale rural food production. Mexico has twenty-five thousand basic goods outlets, with plans for thirty thousand *tiendas bienestar*, well-being stores, by 2030.

We needn't look overseas for inspiration. The US federal government already buys food and sells it directly—at cost—to consumers. The Defense Commissary Agency is often cited as the US government's prime retail outlet, an Uncle Sam's Club with storefronts on over two hundred military bases worldwide and over $5 billion in annual revenue.

Government-run grocery stores that operate at cost can certainly save consumers money—"from twenty to thirty percent," according to Errol Schweizer, former vice president of grocery at Whole Foods (pre-Amazon take-over). But Schweizer suggested to me over email that the idea would need to go still further, "to have a public supply chain, which can internalize the fixed costs of grocery retail—inflation, occupancy and taxes—while ensuring workers are unionized and dignified."

A public supply chain means the city would buy food directly from producers, own or lease warehouses and retail space, and manage distribution. By cutting out private wholesalers, landlords, and shareholders, it can stabilize prices against inflation, avoid commercial rent hikes, and reinvest surpluses rather than extracting them as profit. Crucially, it also sets standards for union wages and dignified work, ensuring that affordable food doesn't come at the expense of exploited labor. It's a win for growers, workers, and eaters and, as a result, it's a coalition-building machine.

Mamdani's plan proposes to invest $60 million in five grocery stores, one per borough. That's not nearly ambitious enough to generate the kind of impact a public grocery program needs. What would be? Schweizer and I figured you would need a minimum of twenty medium-sized stores in the most deprived neighborhoods to achieve economies of scale, with a low inventory count and high union wages. It would cost $400 million a year, many times Mamdani's proposal, but still less than four percent of the NYPD's spending in 2024—and a mere 0.38 percent of the city's entire budget.

But $400 million is still a substantial chunk of change, and it's worth spending a moment to think about the problems a municipal grocery store is designed to solve. They're certainly a way to make it easier for people to buy good food. By opening stores in areas that commercial grocers won't serve, the city can work to eliminate "food deserts," low-income census tracts far from medium-sized grocery stores. (Activists prefer the term "food apartheid," which brings politics back in to name the racialized disinvestment and structural inequality that makes it hard to buy food in low-income neighborhoods.)

That infrastructure will help New Yorkers eat better, but it's not enough: research shows that having a neighborhood grocery store selling good food increases healthy food consumption by only ten percent. Accessibility matters, but affordability matters just as much. That's where one of the perks of a publicly owned supply chain comes in: It can reduce the price of healthy staples like legumes and vegetables, which have recently hit a thirty-five-year low for domestic availability. Lower prices would help drive consumption on their own, but we can expand our horizons even further.

There are a wealth of other policies—junk-food taxes, education to vitiate the food industry's propaganda, restrictions on advertising, and improved school meals—that, working in tandem with a public supply chain, would improve the well-being of all New Yorkers. All these policies rest on a recognition that a community might be made healthier through collective political action against the food industry, and that a grocery store might be an anchor for it.

Many in the food policy community celebrated when Trump gave RFK Jr. carte blanche to "go wild" on corporate abuses in the food chain. Some nutritionists and public health advocates like Marion Nestle, otherwise critical of the administration and RFK Jr., were pleased that the language of sensible public health interventions had finally emerged from the Department of Health and Human Services.

For a moment, it seemed as if the administration's aggressive posture toward food companies—one conspicuously lacking in the Obama and Biden administrations' more supine approach to Big Food—would mark a rare instance where the right was more willing to tackle corporate power than their Democratic counterparts. Compare Make America Healthy Again's lofty ambitions, for instance, to Michelle Obama's organic garden at the White House, a project that at best was a memorial for the "hope and change" in the food system that died on contact with the administration's donors.

But if hopes were misplaced in Obama, they are further misplaced in Trump. Despite its hymns to transparency, his Presidential Commission to Make America Healthy Again is troublingly vague. Its charter document offers a lengthy catalogue of America's public health failings, on which most reasonable people could agree are real and in dire need of structural remedy—for instance, that "the US had the highest age-standardized incidence rate of cancer in 2021, nearly double the next-highest rate." But the document goes on to describe its task as helping Americans manage their exposures to disease and danger by "informing the American people using transparent and clear facts."

The Commission takes a well-founded concern—the opaque and often-compromised connections between corporations and federal bodies charged with governing those corporations—and flips it into a simple call for consumer education. Lately, even the meek transparency goal seems to have been abandoned. In his initial video message to the Department of Health and Human Services, RFK Jr. promised to usher in an era of "radical transparency" as a way to rebuild trust with the American people. Within two months, the entire public records staff at the CDC, FDA, and NIH had been fired. Now, consumers will be alone in taking responsibility for whether or not they fall victim to corporate malfeasance.

The toxic corporate food environment itself will remain largely unchanged, save for cosmetic differences:

By the end of next year, a few petroleum-based colorings will be removed from food products, bringing the US a bit more in line with the rest of the planet. But that kind of regulation is the exception, not the rule. The latest MAHA Commission on Children's Health recommends tackling the problem of pesticide overuse and toxicity not by restricting pesticides, but—again—by educating the public on the EPA's review process. MAHA is, in other words, little more than a germophobe's guide to health care.

Rather than, say, taking on the industry responsible for formulating, marketing, and then inflating the costs of unhealthy food, citizens will have to take it upon themselves to address and manage their exposure. MAHA's stock in trade is biomonitoring devices, blood tests, and mail-in stool samples—all services available for a fee—so that vigilant individuals can avoid the worst. "*You* are the primary person responsible for understanding your body," says the website of Casey Means, the MAHA figurehead currently under consideration for the position of Surgeon General.

The administration has responded to MAHA, in other words, as an enlightened personal-responsibility consumerism. The task of maintaining your purity is yours alone. Talk about regulating the sources of environmental toxins is discouraged. It's not surprising, then, that RFK's plans have spawned dissent among the ranks of the MAHA faithful, many of whom genuinely thought there'd be a chance to do more than remove odd food colorings from Froot Loops. Marion Nestle has already identified MAHA's reluctance to regulate, and more of MAHA are coming to share her dismay.

Meanwhile, MAHA has cast the most promising health programs, particularly for the working class, into darkness. The administration has already cut $1 billion from local food purchasing and millions from regional food business grants, and it has removed millions from SNAP, which helps poor families extend their budgets with healthy foods.

MAHA's crisis presents an opportunity for Mamdani. His right-wing critics, featured in the *New York Times* and on Fox, have suggested that public markets are indications of "communism." Were the Mamdani administration to open twenty unionized Costco-style stores with sustainable, locally produced food, the vituperative and voluble reaction would certainly be greater.

Yet the scale of the attacks on Mamdani reflects the resonance his campaign holds with a New York public sick of food-price inflation that has surpassed the national average for over a decade. A public grocery system—visible, reliable, dignified—can prefigure something larger: collective infrastructures of care that meet immediate needs, exposing the bankruptcy of consumerist fixes.

Those collective expectations, the horizons of political possibility, are the huge stakes at play in today's debate over food. Public grocery's success and failure will be a measure not so much of logistics as of Mamdani's ability to lead a bloc around the vision that it anchors. Grocery stores are not just a venue for food retail but an opportunity to recruit and rearticulate a series of political alliances that, increasingly, feel betrayed by the federal government.

Moms Across America, an organization whose political wing supported MAHA candidates, is already chafing at the administration's capitulation to the pesticide industry and HHS's timidity in addressing the harms wrought by environmental toxins. A public food system would be far readier to regulate, and eliminate, these kinds of poisons from the supply chain, and far more amenable to reasonable scientific debate around protecting children's health from the private food industry. In other words, there's a fraction of the bourgeoisie ready to be recruited to a working-class bloc.

In New York City, the coalition for a public food system is closer to forming than it looks. Community Kitchen has opened at the Lower Eastside Girls Club, joining the wave of efforts to make food a public good rather than a private commodity. The restaurant will offer tiered pricing, so that foodies looking to try James Beard Award cooking will pay $125 to break Mark Bittman's bread with local residents who will pay $15 for the same privilege. This is what a historic bloc might look like in microcosm, led by the working class with elements of the bourgeoisie along for the ride.

Labor is on board, too. Faye Guenther, president of United Food and Commercial Workers 3000, talked about the importance of bringing in the already existing public-sector worker networks. Liz Accles, executive director of Community Food Advocates, a New York City–based nonprofit that drives systemic food justice through policy and coalition building, is optimistic. The City of New York's government spends $500 million a year on food. Public stores could leverage that purchasing power, Accles told me by email, as "a critically important element of a more comprehensive approach to address the lack of quality, affordable grocery access in New York City."

New York's socialist and anarchist movements, the original incubators of the idea of public groceries, are already circling the same demands. Stitch these actors together with unions and public-restaurant pioneers, and what emerges is not just a campaign for cheaper groceries but a counter-hegemonic bloc—multiracial, feminist, immigrant, queer—ready to reclaim food as a public good.

The pieces of a united front are there. Put them together, and you begin to see the outlines of a counter-hegemonic bloc. Public grocery is not a technocratic tweak but a rallying point, a chance to turn discontent into solidarity. Those Spanish socialists railing against philanthropy were right. They wanted low prices, social solidarity, and dignity. Mamdani's vision, if writ large, can durably achieve all three.

FIX OUR SCHOOLS

EDUCATION'S UNTAPPED POTENTIAL

THARMAN SHANMUGARATNAM

LET ME START WITH WHAT I BELIEVE TO BE the two big questions around education and its potential to act as a leveler and shape a better society.

First, we can no longer be confident that meritocratic systems will blunt the advantages and disadvantages that children bring with them from their homes and social backgrounds, at least not in the way they did in a past era. In many countries, we see increasing polarization rather than leveling of achievements according to social backgrounds—in education, jobs, and lifetime incomes.

Second, and critically important, we have to ask how current education systems, already poorly fitted to the needs of today's labor markets, can prepare young people for a new era of work and help them meet their aspirations. It's not the first time we are experiencing technological change, but we know that the nature and spread of technology's impact on jobs will be different as artificial intelligence becomes increasingly potent.

It is too early to have a confident read on which jobs and human tasks AI will displace and which complementary or new jobs will emerge, but we must expect it to impact a broader swathe of middle-class jobs, including many more white-collar jobs, than did previous waves of automation. Those are the jobs that much of today's post-secondary education seeks to prepare people for.

We have to address these phase shifts—one in the way social backgrounds are increasingly shaping outcomes in life and the other in the way a more powerful form of digital automation will impact jobs and possibly usher in broader insecurity in the years to come. The combination of the two will be toxic. It will undermine faith in meritocracy itself and in the ability of both the state and markets to give everyone a fair chance of success. It's a future that we have to avoid.

How we invest in and organize education has to be at the core of how we tackle these challenges. Indeed, what ails education, particularly in highly decentralized systems like that in the US, is that we have left it too much to the social and economic marketplace.

The market is not socially neutral. It practices its own forms of "social engineering." It starts with assortative mating, with better-educated individuals marrying one another—that's been on the rise almost everywhere. It continues with the much larger investments that well-off parents make in their children, beginning in critical early years. That shift has been well documented in the US—the way higher-educated and better-off parents do more to prepare their kids to get into the best preschools, spending much more on enrichment activities, and just spending more time with them.

It continues also in the tendency toward socially segregated neighborhoods. Studies of the US experience have thrown light on how neighborhoods matter, in tangible and intangible ways. As neighborhoods become increasingly different, so do schools, and the way teachers are sorted between schools in decentralized systems tends to reinforce the effects of social sorting of students. Finally, these differences in how children grow up is compounded in employment markets, with top-tier employers hiring excessively from the most prestigious universities or based on social pedigree.

Nevertheless, there are several reasons for believing that education has significant untapped potential as a leveler. The first is that we have yet to achieve scale in quality early interventions, beginning with maternal health and continuing for children up to the age of three. This requires public resources, better-trained professionals, and active community involvement.

While the evidence is not water-tight, the weight of expert opinion points to quality interventions at this early stage as being the most effective way to uplift life chances among children born into disadvantage and yielding a significant social return. Scaling them up is an opportunity.

The second reason for optimism lies precisely in the divergent outcomes we see across geographies, systems, and social backgrounds. It means there is scope for leveling up. We see that school systems in different countries have diverse achievement levels and degrees of social mobility. There must surely be scope to adapt and assimilate some of the best practices of systems internationally and achieve some convergence.

In the same vein, for the same socioeconomic profile, the significant differences in educational achievement and social mobility outcomes within countries depending on where you grew up illustrate the scope for policies and institutions to close the gaps. Even the fact that children from well-off families are doing much better than before and that the gap between them and poorer children has widened shows what is possible. The relationship between income and achievement is not immutable.

A third reason stems from the significant inefficiencies in tertiary education, in a wide range of countries. There is a large mismatch between the demand and supply of skills, particularly for jobs in the broad middle. There is also a mismatch between the types of abilities of students and the pathways they're taking in tertiary education. If we can reduce these mismatches, we unlock significant human capital.

Fourth, there's still a large opportunity to invest in systems of lifelong learning. We are still far from making it the norm for people from all segments of the workforce—not just knowledge professionals—to get regular injections of knowhow and skills so they can keep growing over the course of their careers. We have to achieve that in order to arrest the common pattern of blue-collar and average white-collar wages stagnating once people hit middle age, while the upper end of the wage scale continues to grow.

There's a lot more to be done, and reasons to avoid being pessimistic about education's potential. However, they require fundamental policy rethinking in a number of regards. We have to rethink higher education if we are to reduce the large mismatch of skills in labor markets and better develop the potential of a whole spectrum of young people.

We have taken the college premium too simplistically and shaped too much policy and politics around it.

Encouraging more high school graduates to go to college is not going to earn them the college premium. The premium commonly cited is an average, but the distribution around the average deserves greater light of day. It has long been the case that those in the bottom quintile of college graduates in the US earn a quite small premium over high school graduates. That's among those who graduate; in fact, forty percent of those who enroll in universities in the US don't complete a degree within six years. Of those who do, a substantial proportion—some forty percent—do not end up working at jobs that require a college degree. Graduate underemployment is likewise widespread in parts of Asia, such as India.

The real question for young people, and for public policy, is not whether they should stop after high school or go on to college. It must be about the form of tertiary education—academic or applied, traditional or dual/co-operative, two-year or four-year—that will best secure a skills premium and help them climb a ladder of skills in their careers.

We have over-expanded the traditional, academically oriented model of tertiary education in too many countries and need to rebalance in favor of applied learning. The theory of change is that people discover their abilities and interests when they do something applied. This does not mean we should focus their learning on specific or hard skills. We have to develop in them the broader set of soft and hard skills that will enable them to keep adapting throughout their lives.

But neither can it be said that a traditional or liberal arts education is the only way, or even the best way, to develop soft skills such as creativity, teamwork, and cross-cultural skills. We can and must pay attention to developing these skills through the applied route as well.

Lifelong learning has become a mantra everywhere, but we have a long way to go. It requires strong tripartite and other social partnerships to work well. We have to recognize, however, that there is a difference in the motivations and incentives of firms and workers. Firms typically want to focus training on skills specific to their own needs. Workers have the incentive to pick up skills that help them develop their careers—which will inevitably take them to other employers or even other sectors.

In Denmark, most training is supported by employers

but conducted by public institutions. People are able to attend a course they desire, even if it doesn't match their employer's immediate needs. In some other northern European countries, however, firm-specific training dominates. We need a balance between the two approaches, even as we step up both.

Above all, we need greater strategic focus in public policy on reskilling and up-skilling workers. Past eras of technological progress led to a movement of labor from low-productivity to high-productivity activities, such as from initially low-productivity agricultural work to manufacturing and later to modern services. That followed Arthur Lewis' description of economic development. Now, we see a reverse Lewisian movement in several advanced economies, with a new wave of digital automation pushing people from relatively higher-productivity manufacturing jobs into lower-productivity and lower-wage services jobs. It's a trend we have to avert.

The most careful studies point to the potential for future tasks and jobs that complement the new technologies, including AI, and for new areas of work to emerge. But whether we get there depends on what we do now—to develop coalitions of industry, government bodies, unions, and educational institutions that anticipate new job demands in each sector and curate programs that enable people to develop new skills and stay in a high-productivity sphere of activity. We've got to get on with it.

LEARN TO GRIEVE

SARAH JAFFE

GRIEF IS A NECESSARY PART OF LIFE, A painful yet transformative experience that deserves its space and time and respect and care. But the amount of misery, the violence and cruelty of this world, the premature death all around us—this is not necessary. This, I think, we can change. The radical project is to accept that death and grief are inevitable but not let that be an excuse to ignore all the preventable horrors, or rather to be motivated to tell the difference between the inevitability of mortality and the brutality of racial capitalism.

A transformative politics, then, a socialism or communism worth the name, would be interested in expanding the range of "emotional freedom" alongside the material, because it would recognize the two as intertwined. The realm of emotional freedom begins where the realm of necessity ends; we must have time and our needs met in order to experience the rich spectrum of emotions that come with a full and connected life. We could protect one another's vulnerability while accepting the inevitability of that vulnerability, able to risk more emotional entanglements precisely because our bodily survival is assured.

Caring for one another is part of this process. Becoming a caregiver teaches us that there is something desperately wrong with the way capitalist society allocates value and time. It insists that we make friends with our mortality. I cannot honestly write here that I have made peace with mine. At times it leaves me breathless, panicked, still. I have the ordinary vanities of a woman in her forties, aware that the world around me places different value on an aging woman.

Grief still tears me apart at times. But it has taught me patience that I never had and acceptance of a strange kind; it has allowed me to see the way the people around me show up for me, to recognize the ways I am loved. To let go of my desire for control. Grief has taught me to live with the knowledge that I can be undone at any moment, and to live alongside the fear.

As I have aged, I have had to become comfortable with the idea that I may not live to see the better world I work to bring about. That the struggle does not depend on any one person is something I have long known; it is a knowledge that has brought me a kind of peace. On my bedroom wall hangs a print that reads, "Do not be daunted by the enormity of the world's grief. You are not obligated to complete the work, but neither are you free to abandon it." It is a line from Jewish rabbinical teachings, and it reminds me that I am one of many, that the struggle continues without me.

The value of all the lives around me, before me and after me—not in some hypothetical calculable way but the connections that I can see, my young niece as she sings at the top of her lungs the words of musicians who are her grandmother's age—this is what keeps me going. We are always, in one sense or another, salvaging something from the brief time that we have. People will always get sick and die. We will break each other's hearts; we will move and change. Grief is inevitable. It is part of what it means to be human. Only in a society that makes no room for this reality does grief become revolutionary.

Because we live in a time when the gap between promise and fulfillment is so large, when the state offers nothing but cruelty and walls and closes its eyes to our illness, rationalizes mass death, and capital picks up shop and leaves us unable to pay our way, when the natural world itself seems to be seeking revenge, we are, I think, feeling particularly vulnerable.

We are constantly imagining the end of the world and worrying about the end of the month. In this time we have a choice: to cling to crumbling structures that will collapse and bury us, or to hold on to each other while we pick our way through the rubble. We can mourn as we build something else.

I think of Palestinian people in Gaza, pulling one another from the rubble left by Israeli bombs. I am haunted, like, I think, everyone who saw it, by a video of a young girl on a stretcher carried by several men. She asks them, "Am I being taken to the cemetery?" and one of the men replies, "No, love, here you are, you're alive, and beautiful like the moon!"

I return again and again to the defiant insistence on life, on beauty amid the ruins, the word so many of us learned as we counted days and then weeks and then months of destruction: *sumud*, steadfastness, through horrors that most of my readers will never suffer. Hala Alyan explained, "The idea of *sumud* has become a multifaceted cultural concept among Palestinians: it means steadfastness, a derivative of *arranging* or *saving up*, even *adorning*. It implies composure braided with rootedness, a posture that might bend but will not break."

The people we meet amid the ruins may not be the ones we would have chosen. I do not know if the man in the video knew the girl he comforted, only that he did it with practiced care. We may be hailed by our neighbors, co-workers, the person we pass on the street who asks for a favor, a coin, a hand. One of the challenges of building a politics for collapse is that working across difference is hard. It requires patience and forgiveness and generosity and learning. It requires care for the immediate needs of others and also for the needs that span generations. It requires this kind of composure amid destruction, to salvage what we can.

After this kind of rupture the future is uncertain, as is the map from here to there. But people have done it before, risked everything to make a better world, and sometimes they have even succeeded.

I think our struggles will be about homes and care and the thing we call "supply chains" but that are in fact people doing work. They will be about removing bottlenecks in access to basic needs and about surviving the floods and fires and bombs. They will be about who will pay for capitalist destruction. They will be about forcing the powerful to concede something to the rest of us.

The struggles will generate fierce opposition: fascists and the rest of the far right and even ordinary neoliberalism will resist giving up their resource hoards as fiercely as any fairy-tale dragon, even when those hoards are fairy tales as well.

There are way stations being built in the ruins right

now. In Minneapolis, Inquilinxs Unidxs Por Justicia has its housing cooperative and its office building on George Floyd Square. Their work is a process, Jen Arnold told me, of building pieces of the world they want to see along the way, of building material infrastructures of resistance that then can expand.

Sisters Uncut occupied an empty council flat in Hackney, East London, bringing together the community to work on collective solutions to "Islamophobic street attacks, harassment by transphobes, beatings by abusive partners, assaults by cops, and violent evictions," all the everyday dehumanizations of life at this point on the clock of capitalism.

It was messy and confrontational, but it built something new. This is the everyday making of abolition, of making the world in the conditions we were given, not the ones we chose.

In Puerto Rico, Xiomara Caro Díaz was also thinking about the kinds of organizations that could hold failure and loss and grief. The kinds of movements that have space to dance and that have support for people to step away when they need to mourn. She dreamed, she told me, of organizing a march of the dead. To let go of the idea that you can solve everything by endless work, she suggested, might make it more likely that you figure out how to change something.

Working in the ruins requires an ability to admit when things are not working, when they have failed. In a world full of expectations of endless progress, it can feel impossible to admit to setbacks and disappointments, but learning from loss is necessary. An organization that holds space for people to just be people is more likely not to lose its members when they face loss.

The work that I saw in Puerto Rico, in London, in Minneapolis, and elsewhere was taking place in what Rodrigo Nunes called a movement ecology. Each group had in different ways accepted a version of Caro's insight, acting on a piece of the problem and thereby expanding the possibilities for others, in their neighborhoods and in the world.

In Minneapolis, tenant organizers and labor organizers shared space and joined the street uprising and the precinct occupation, unions financially supported community organizations, and teachers joined their students in protests. Thinking ecologically is not only thinking about the needs of the planet but also thinking about the relationships we already have and the ones we want to build, the way our political and economic actions affect one another. Thinking of ourselves and others not as leaders and followers but as people who at any time might lead and always have something to learn.

Admitting we do not know the answers—that I certainly do not—we can nevertheless make what Nunes called "strategic wagers," educated guesses as to what types of action will connect with the most people, where the pressure points can be.

The path ahead is bumpy and full of twists around which we cannot see and events we cannot control. In moments of uprising, of mass strikes and rebellions, we construct new paths and new connections, new forms of consciousness, even that nebulous thing called "class consciousness." If you have come this far with me and still flinch at this word, consider that the week I wrote this, before the United Auto Workers went on strike, an Australian capitalist called publicly for "pain in the economy" to "remind people that they work for the employer, not the other way around."

What this capitalist called "arrogance" in the labor market was only the earliest sprout, post-pandemic, of a real class consciousness, but he was determined to root it out. (He later apologized, but his is not a rare view, only rare in how bluntly and publicly he expressed it.)

The capitalists already have class consciousness; they always have. Because capital requires a group that is subjugated, a lesser caste. Their vision of the world is the world as it is, only we grovel more.

So let's dream of a world otherwise. Such dreams are born in moments of rupture; they are inspired by loss. They are emotional as well as intellectual, irrational in their beauty. They come amid the flames and floodwaters, in conversations in police vans. They come, as Saidiya Hartman wrote, from "waywardness and the refusal to be governed."

From moments of excess and overwhelm, from insisting on living in the ruins. Grief is excessive; so is revolution. It is a defiant yes when the rest of the world would say no. It is a refusal of the foreclosing of our time, an overflowing of humanity into the places where it is forbidden. We will not be machines anymore.

That such visions are born from ruin is, I think, what makes them possible. It is a salvage communism we can imagine now (a term that I take from the *Salvage* magazine collective). It is a project of world-making from the pieces that we have been left.

Walter Benjamin at his most messianic understood that what I have called grief time is a pause that contains endless possibility. Our time is filled with so much bullshit, but grief time, in my experience, while it enveloped me in fog also seemed to tear away the spell that made bullshit seem worthwhile. I wanted, rather than to rebuild the cracked foundations, to blast the whole thing to hell.

I want to return to love as I close. I want to return to the people I found in the wreckage of my life and the people who held out their scarred hands to me from my past. After I finished writing I went for a walk and bought supplies for Rosh Hashanah—because it was, that evening, the Jewish New Year—and had a wander through the parts of South London I love the most.

I paused in a park where I had gone first with a person who has been picking up pieces of me since he met me, and

I sat on a bench and hit shuffle on the playlist that I made for this book, and the song that came up was called "Be and Bring Me Home," and I thought of what it means to be home, what it means to miss someone, the difference between heartache and heartbreak and grief. And because the universe is perverse and sometimes magic, I looked at my phone as I left the park, and he had texted me a heart and an apology for something infinitesimally small in the scale of the rubble we have walked through together.

ACKNOWLEDGMENTS

"Defend Diversity" originally appeared in *The Nation* as "They're Not Just Coming for DEI. They're Coming for Democracy." Copyright © 2025 by Stacey Abrams. Reprinted by permission of *The Nation*; "Embrace Clean Energy" excerpted from HERE COMES THE SUN: A LAST CHANCE FOR THE CLIMATE AND A FRESH CHANCE FOR CIVILIZATION by Bill McKibben. Copyright © 2025 by Bill McKibben. Used by permission of W.W. Norton and Company, Inc.; "Recognize Entropy" excerpted from *Entropy Economics: The Living Basis of Value and Production*, by James K. Galbraith and Jing Chen, University of Chicago Press, 2025; "Resist Media Consolidation" originally appeared on *The Ankler* as "The WBD Deal Puts Hollywood, and Democracy, at Risk." Copyright © 2025 by Jane Fonda. Reprinted courtesy of the author. Originally published on *The Ankler* on December 4, 2025; "Ditch Neoliberalism" excerpted from THE ROAD TO FREEDOM: ECONOMICS AND THE GOOD SOCIETY by Joseph E. Stiglitz. Copyright © 2024 by Joseph E. Stiglitz. Used by permission of W.W. Norton and Company, Inc. "Create a Healthy Economy" originally published as "Our Sick

Economy," *American Prospect*, © 2026, prospect.org; "Redistribute" excerpted from *Enshittification: Why Everything Suddenly Got Worse and What to Do About It,* by Cory Doctorow, Farrar, Straus and Giroux, 2025; "Reject Techno-fixes" adapted from *Against Platforms: Surviving Digital Utopia,* by Mike Pepi; "Tax the Rich" excerpted from *The Second Estate: How the Tax Code Made an American Aristocracy*, by Ray D. Madoff, University of Chicago Press, 2025; “"Resist Billionaires" adapted from *Burned by Billionaires: How Concentrated Wealth and Power Are Ruining Our Lives and Planet.* Copyright © 2025 by Chuck Collins; Reprinted by permission of The New Press. www.thenewpress.org ; "Resist Nationalism" excerpted from *Border and Rule: Global Migration, Capitalism, and the Rise of Racist Nationalism*, by Harsha Walia, 2001, Haymarket Press; "Control Your Food" excerpted from an original article, "MAHA vs. Mamdani," that appeared in the *Boston Review*, September 17, 2025; "Fix Our Schools" excerpted from Tharman Shanmugaratnam, "Education's Untapped Potential," in Olivier Blanchard and Dani Rodrik, eds., *Combating Inequality: Rethinking Government's Role*, ©

2021 Massachusetts Institute of Technology and Peterson Institute for International Economics, by permission of the MIT Press; "Learn to Grieve" excerpted from *From the Ashes: Grief and Revolution in a World on Fire*, by Sarah Jaffe, Bold Type Books, copyright 2024.

CONTRIBUTORS

STACEY ABRAMS, the Democratic nominee for governor of Georgia in 2018 and 2022, is the founder of American Pride Rises, a group dedicated to defending the principles of diversity, equity, and inclusion.

JING CHEN teaches finance at the University of Northern British Columbia.

CORY DOCTOROW is a science fiction novelist, journalist, and author of *Enshittification: Why Everything Suddenly Got Worse and What to Do About It*.

JANE FONDA is an Oscar– and Emmy award–winning American actress and a political activist. She is the leader of the Committee for the First Amendment, an organization that defends freedom of expression from political interference and censorship.

JAMES K. GALBRAITH holds the Lloyd M. Bentsen Jr. Chair in government/business relations at the Lyndon B. Johnson School of Public Affairs at the University of Texas.

M. GESSEN is an Opinion columnist for the *New York Times*. They won a George Polk Award for opinion writing in 2024 and the Pulitzer Prize for opinion writing in 2026. They are the author of eleven books, including *The Future Is History: How Totalitarianism Reclaimed Russia*, which won the National Book Award in 2017.

SARAH JAFFE, a writer and reporter living in London, is also a columnist at *The Progressive*.

KIM KELLY is a writer and radical organizer that connects worker struggles and the current state of the American labor movement with its storied—and sometimes bloodied—past. She is the author of *Fight Like Hell: The Untold History of American Labor.*

RAY D. MADOFF is a professor at Boston College Law School and co-founder and director of the Boston College Forum on Philanthropy and the Public Good.

BILL MCKIBBEN is the author of *The End of Nature* and twenty other books. He is the Schumann Distinguished Scholar at Middlebury College.

HAROLD MEYERSON is an editor-at-large for the *American Prospect* and a former opinion columnist for the *Washington Post.*

RAJ PATEL is a research professor at the Lyndon B. Johnson School of Public Affairs at the University of Texas and author of *The Value of Nothing.*

BERNIE SANDERS has served in the US Senate since 2007.

THARMAN SHANMUGARATNAM is president of the Republic of Singapore.

REBECCA SOLNIT is a *Guardian* US columnist. She is the author of *Orwell's Roses* and co-editor with Thelma Young Lutunatabua of the climate anthology *Not Too Late: Changing the Climate Story from Despair to Possibility*.

JOSEPH E. STIGLITZ is a public policy analyst, political activist, and professor at Columbia University. He won the Nobel Memorial Prize in Economic Sciences in 2001.

HARSHA WALIA is an activist and writer based in Vancouver. In 2001, she co-founded No One Is Illegal, an anti-capitalist migrant justice movement.